TREES
FOR FLOWER AND FRAGRANCE

MELALEUCA laterita

TREES
FOR FLOWER AND FRAGRANCE

A-Z GARDENING SERIES

STIRLING MACOBOY

THE BOOK COMPANY

ACKNOWLEDGEMENTS

The flowering trees in this book were photographed
In Australia
At Adelaide Botanic Gardens; Brisbane, Botanic Gardens and the Oasis Park; Bendigo, Maryborough and Melbourne, Victoria; Abbotsleigh College, Bellingen, Botany Bay, Bowral, Camellia Grove, Chatswood Memorial Park, Four Seasons Nursery, Lindfield Park, Milton Park, the Royal Botanic Gardens, Stony Range Reserve and Yowie Bay, all in NSW; and in Canberra, ACT.
In the United States
At Arnold Arboretum and Jamaica Pond, Mass.; Foster Gardens, Kapiolani Park, the Lyon Arboretum and Pua Laki, Hawaii; the Descanso Gardens, Huntingdon Gardens, La Brea Park, Los Angeles State and County Arboretum, Roger Reynolds Nursery, South Coast Botanic Garden, Strybing Arboretum, Sunset Gardens and UCLA Botanic Gardens in California.

In Europe
Jardin des Plantes Paris, and Malmaison, France; Prague Botanic Garden; RAF College, Cranwell, Kew Gardens and RHS Gardens, Wisley, U.K.
In Asia
Manila Botanic Garden, Makiling, Rizal Park and University of the Philippines; Shinjuku Go-en, Tokyo; Singapore Botanic Garden.
In the Pacific
Hotels Bora Bora, Taaone, Tahara'a and Tahiti, Jardin Botanique de Tahiti, all in French Polynesia; Pago Pago, American Samoa; Avarua, Rarotonga.
My thanks to the unknown gardeners in whose homes many of the best trees were found; to the many garden-minded friends who brought individual trees to my attention and who helped with the transport and notetaking.
All photographs by the author except *Nuytsia floribunda*, page 118, by Reg Morrison.

Opposite page: Thevetia thevetioides.

THE BOOK COMPANY

*This edition published and distributed by
The Book Company International
9/9–13 Winbourne Road
Brookvale 2100, Sydney NSW Australia*

*This edition published in 1994
in conjunction with Lansdowne Publishing Pty Ltd
Level 5, 70 George Street Sydney NSW 2000, Australia
Managing Director: Jane Curry
Production Manager: Sally Stokes*

*This book is copyright.
Apart from any fair dealing for the purposes of private study, research, criticism or review, as permitted under the Copyright Act, no part may be reproduced by any process without written permission. Inquiries should be addressed to the publishers.*

*First published by Lansdowne Press, Sydney, in 1982
Reprinted by Angus & Robertson Publishers in 1989
Reprinted by The Book Company 1994.*

Copyright © Stirling Macoboy 1982

*National Library of Australia
Cataloguing-in-publication data.*

*Macoboy, Stirling, 1927–
  Trees for flower and fragrance.*

  *Includes index.
  ISBN 1 86302 354 2.*

  *1. Flowering trees. 2. Gardens, Fragrant. I. Title.
  (Series: Macoboy, Stirling, 1927– . A-Z gardening series).*

635.9'77

Line drawings by Murray Frederick

Printed in Singapore by Tien Wah Press (Pte) Ltd

CONTENTS

INTRODUCTION
· **6** ·

PLANT A TREE
HELP SAVE A WORLD!
· **7** ·

HOW TO GROW FLOWERING TREES
· **8** ·

HOW TO USE THIS BOOK
· **11** ·

DICTIONARY OF FLOWERING TREES
· **13** ·

INDEX
· **156** ·

FLOWERING TREES

INTRODUCTION

An average garden has room for only 5 or 6 trees at most — so it is important to choose the right ones! Any tree will provide precious shade and shelter; but surely that tree is twice blessed if it also produces a seasonal display of blossom to satisfy the aesthetic side of our natures. The flower is not merely a source of beauty to human admirers, but the tree's method of reproduction. By attracting fertilizing insects it is transformed into decorative fruits which make up directly or indirectly part of the diet of every living creature. These fruits (whether they are acorns, beans, berries, drupes, pods, pomes or whatever) contain the seed which is the beginning of life for a new generation of the tree. The birds that eat the berries excrete the seeds that grow into new trees.

But this only happens when the birds themselves make our gardens their home, and they only do this with an ample supply of bloom from which to sip nectar. Every garden, then, can come to life through the inclusion of at least one flowering tree, say as the focal point of its design. But be sure it is one suited to your soil conditions and climatic range. We may fall in love with a Poinciana on a visit to the tropics and decide to plant one. It will probably grow (for trees are very adaptable) but it will never bloom without the heat and humidity of the tropical wet season. One of my neighbours has one; he's been waiting at least 30 years and hasn't seen a bloom yet.

It's the same story if you live in a warm winter area and fancy Dogwood. Without the cold, it just won't put on a display at all — and without flowers there are no berries; without berries, no new Dogwoods . . .

This book will not only show you a vast range of flowering trees that bloom magnificently in the right climate. The accompanying text will tell you what that climate is, the position the tree likes, its size and season of growth. You'll learn how to plant it, how to prune it, how to care for it.

The choice is wide, wherever you live, and we hope this book will help you make it.

Magnolia veitchii ▶

Plant a Tree Help Save a World!

Since time immemorial, trees have been the most prominent living feature of any natural setting away from the polar regions of the earth. They are the backbone of life as we know it, for they conserve water, control pollution, protect the very earth itself. They are the oxygen banks, the air cleaners, the rain-bringers and erosion preventers of nature. They are also her most beautiful creation.

Almost every aspect of our life is in some way influenced by trees. They bring us shade, shelter and privacy; their wood builds our houses, our bridges and boats. Their fruits help feed and furnish and comfort us; their dead tissue has been transformed over the ages into the fossil fuels of coal and gas and oil that keep the wheels of industry turning, grant us the blessings of fire and warmth, make it possible for us to be transported in comfort by land, by sea, by air. Trees supply us indirectly with everything in life, yet for generations we have cut them down without replacement, without a thought for the future that seems so far off, yet is so dangerously close.

Already, entire regions have been denuded of their natural forests, and the resulting atmospheric pollution of carbon dioxide (which trees would have converted into life-giving oxygen) is causing great concern. Scientists believe this is causing dangerous changes in the world climate which could ultimately spell out the end of man's reign on earth.

If we are tree lovers as we claim, we must replant now, and continually, to help redress the damage already done to our soil, our climate, our wild life, our entire ecology. For what chance does a single tree (or even a whole race of trees) stand, when measured against the apathy of politicians, the greed of land developers, the short-sightedness of farmers?

Each and every one of us must speak out *now* for the protection and replacement of the trees that were once around us. The trees without which our civilization could never have risen to its present heights — and without which it certainly has no future.

Stirling Macoboy
Neutral Bay, N.S.W.

How to Grow Flowering Trees

Whichever flowering tree you've chosen to beautify your garden, and wherever you decide to place it, correct planting and maintenance will guarantee swift, even growth and a long, colourful span of years.

WHEN TO PLANT A TREE

Modern nursery practice is to sell all young trees ready-growing in containers, so they can be planted out any time of year without risk of loss. They will, however, grow faster, with minimum transplant shock, if certain basic rules are followed. Completely deciduous trees are best set out in late winter or very early spring, when bare and dormant. Evergreen trees from cold or temperate climates do best when planted in mid-autumn so the roots have time to get established before cold weather halts growth, or in mid-spring with the sap in full flow and a full season's growth ahead of them. The main exceptions are trees from distinctly tropical climates which are customarily planted in warm (even hot) weather, with appropriate care and water so they do not dehydrate.

Ornamental trees for garden use are expensive items — you are paying not only for the tree itself, but for the time and labour incurred in raising it to a suitable size for sale — generally at three or four years of age. Therefore it makes sense to take every possible precaution for its healthy survival.

TESTING FOR DRAINAGE AND DEPTH

The most common cause of failure is incorrect drainage. If water remains around the tree's roots, it will drown. Test the chosen position by digging a hole at least 30cm/12in deep and fill it with water. If water remains in the hole more than 12 hours, you'll need to improve the drainage. This is done by redigging the hole at least 30cm deeper than the young tree's roots will require, and filling in the extra depth with gravel, crushed tile or other draining material. If your pre-planting excavation reveals solid rock less than 50cm/20in below the surface, you'd better choose another planting site. A mature tree's roots need to go way down to support it against wind and supply it with moisture in periods of excessive dryness. When this is the only *possible* position for the tree, however, the difficulty can be overcome by constructing a raised bed with retaining wall to provide the necessary depth of soil.

PREPARING FOR PLANTING

Having decided on a suitable position, dig a hole at least twice the width of the root-ball in the container, and at least 30cm deeper. Professional gardeners would say, the poorer the natural soil, the wider and deeper your hole should be. If you're planting in a lawn, mark out a neat circle about 1m/3ft in diameter, then cut and lift out the circumscribed grass area. Set the grass aside for later use. Lay a sheet of plastic on the lawn nearby, and dig all soil from the hole onto it, until you have reached an adequate depth. Loosen the soil in the bottom of the hole with a garden fork to help drainage.

Now insert a heavy garden stake (treated with preservative) slightly off-centre in the hole and hammer well in. The stake should

PLANTING A TREE

a: *Dig hole, place stake off-centre, partly refill.*

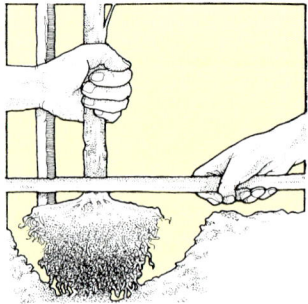

b: *Place tree at correct level, then refill hole.*

c: *Water, then tie trunk to stake, as shown.*

reach at least 1m above soil level, or to the lower branches in the case of a taller tree. Chop up the removed grass-turf and place it around the stake, grass-side down. Mix the removed soil thoroughly with garden compost and sand, and partly fill the hole so the young tree's rootball will be on a level with the surrounding area. Tread the filling firmly so that it is reasonably level.

PLANTING THE TREE

Now, having watered the young tree in its container, place it in position. Do not risk root damage by pulling the tree out of the container. Cut it away with secateurs if plastic, with tin snips if metal. Be sure you finally slide the container base away from under the plant. The whole root ball should now be visible, the tree's container soil level with the surrounding area, or slightly above it. If roots are wound around the perimeter of the ball, they should be gently teased out with a hand fork, and spread radially out across the hole. Add more soil mixture until the hole is three-quarters full; pack down lightly with your foot to get rid of air pockets. Scatter a couple of handfuls of slow-release fertilizer (bone meal is ideal) over the covered root area, then a layer of compost or moistened peat. Add several buckets of water at this time to help settle the soil around the roots. Turn in the balance of the enriched soil — but this time do not tamp. Rake it level, leaving a slight depression away from the trunk to collect water.

Soak the newly planted tree slowly and deeply. Finally, tie the tree firmly to the stake in one or more places. Use a soft material such as hessian or burlap strips that will not cut into the bark. This should first be wound around the stake several times so stake and tree cannot rub together. When several layers thick, the whole can be secured with garden twine or wire. Alternatively, you can buy a proprietary tree tie, which is easier to loosen or remove as the trunk thickens.

If the tree comes already balled in burlap or hessian, place it in position on top of a slight mound in the hole, loosen the ties and leave the burlap in place when you fill in the hole. Roots will grow right through and it will soon rot away. If the tree is balled in plastic, however, this must be completely removed. Balled trees are best supported by guy-wires to prevent their rocking in the wind and loosening young roots. Run the wires through small sections of rubber or plastic hose looped around the trunk and stretch each of them taut to small stakes hammered firmly in around the tree. Three should be enough, at regular spacing.

AFTER CARE FOR NEW TREES

Keep the cleared lawn area around the newly planted tree free of weeds and grass for several years at least, and mulch to a depth of at least 10cm/4in before the hot weather begins in late spring. This will help retain moisture and keep the roots cool. The mulch could be shredded pine bark, lawn clippings, apricot hulls, peat or whatever is commonly available in your area.

The young tree will need regular water at least twice a month for the first two years — the dryness of the soil being the key to frequency. A slow dribbler hose is best, spread around the root area to correspond with the spread of the branches at any time.

Check the ties attaching the tree to the supporting stake in late spring and summer. If they seem tight, loosen them off. It should be possible to remove them, together with

LOPPING A BRANCH

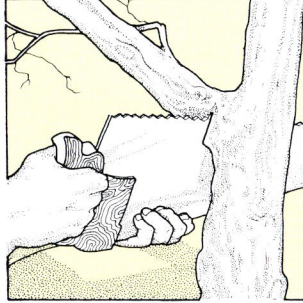

d: *Partly undercut branch, 20cm/8in out from trunk.*

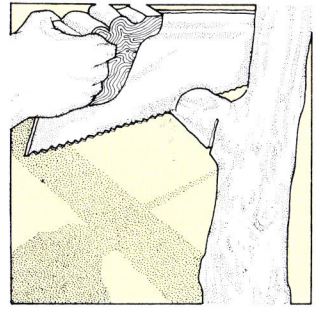

e: *Saw through from above, 10cm/4in beyond first cut.*

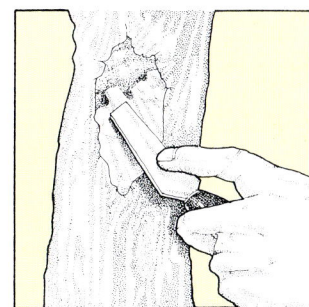

f: *Remove stub flush and paint with tree-wound paint.*

the stake, at the end of two years

FEEDING THE TREE

Young trees need little or no feeding beyond what they pick up from the surrounding mulch. After several years, however, a regular spring feeding will be beneficial. Again, the important area is well out from the trunk beneath the perimeter of the branches. That's where the feeding roots are. Make a number of 20cm/8in deep holes over the root area using a crowbar or similar pointed tool. Through a funnel, half-fill the holes with a slow-release fertilizer formulated for shrub and tree growth. Top up the holes with soil and water deeply.

PRUNING THE TREE

Trees should not be over-pruned: after all, they grow to a shape set by nature. Provided you have chosen a tree that will not outgrow its allotted space, the only reasons for pruning should be (a) to help it get established; (b) to ensure healthy, even growth; (c) to improve yield of fruit or flowers by encouraging the development of multiple flowering twigs. A tree's root mass is usually equivalent to the mass of its branches and foliage. The foliage can therefore evaporate moisture as quickly as the roots can soak it up. If there has been any loss or damage to roots at the time of planting, it is essential to trim the young branches to help balance the loss. Trim your tree, in any case, before new growth starts, forcing the sap to flow in the direction you have chosen. Cut cleanly, with sharp secateurs, any damaged or dead wood, any crossing twigs that may rub, damaging the bark. Trim away young shoots to the height you envisage as exposed trunk (within the first metre initially, to a greater height later on). If thinning out branches, give preference to one of two either directly opposite one another at the same height, or directly above one another on the same side of the tree. The general idea is to encourage a spread of branches spaced equally at various heights, so that rain and sun can reach all parts. Suckers from below graft level must at all times be removed, preferably by tearing them away.

Pruning or lopping of branches too large for your secateurs must always be done in this way: first, make a deep cut with a saw on the *underside* of the branch, at least 20cm/ 8in out from the trunk. Begin a second cut on the top side of the branch, 10cm beyond the first. This time cut right through, and when the branch breaks away, it can strip bark *only* back to the first cut. Finally remove the branch stub parallel with the trunk surface, again cutting from below. This will leave a wound wider than the diameter of the cut branch. Paint or spray the raw surface with an asphalt tree-wound sealer to prevent fungus infection. Within a year or two the bark will grow right over it! Pruning is best done as soon as possible after flower fall.

SEASONAL PROTECTION

In cold climates, where there is regular frost or even snow, the trunks of young trees need protection from frostbite and bark split. This can be assured by wrapping the trunk in strips of burlap at the end of autumn. (The Japanese tie the tree in jackets of bundled straw.) Place a layer of mulch at least 15cm deep over the root area. The same protection (but applied in spring) will protect young trunks and roots from dehydration and sunburn in hot dry areas. Bark is the mature tree's natural protection, but on saplings it is not much thicker than your own skin.

PESTS AND DISEASES

These are generally less troublesome than on smaller plants — but when infestations do occur, they are also more difficult to eradicate due to the tree's bulk and height. Mildew is a universal problem in crowded gardens and in humid weather. It can generally be disregarded on deciduous trees, though spraying with any good fungicide will work wonders if you can reach the infected areas. Caterpillars of all kinds can be as destructive as on smaller plants, and the foliage should be sprayed with Malathion or a similar insecticide on a still day. Make sure you wear glasses and a face mask and don't stand on the lee side of any tree you are spraying. Red spider mite can be a disfiguring pest, especially on ornamental conifers in dry weather. Spray as above, and do what you can to raise humidity by misting foliage, keeping a damp mulch around the tree. Any other disease problems should be discussed with your local agriculture department or nurseryman. But please, take along a specimen of the diseased foliage or bark when you pay them a visit. Just as in human diagnosis, the presence of the patient (or part of it) is essential.

How to Use This Book

All flowering trees included in this book are arranged in the alphabetical order of their botanical names — in some cases, the only names the trees have. These may sometimes be hard to remember, but they have the advantage of being universally understood, which popular names in any modern language are not. If you know the botanical name already, just leaf through the pages until you come to it in alphabetical order. If you know only a popular name, e.g., Horse Chestnut, turn to the comprehensive Index beginning on page 156. Here you will find all commonly used popular names and synonyms, again in alphabetical order, and each popular name will refer you to the plant's botanical name, and to the page on which the entry begins: e.g., Horse Chestnut, see *Aesculus* 16. There are many more popular names than botanical names listed because many tree genera have more than one popular name, or include more than one species, each of which has its own popular name.

Altogether, 331 species of flowering tree are listed and described, together with innumerable varieties. Over 250 of these are illustrated in full colour.

Each entry includes a great deal of useful information, some of it in abbreviated form in the heading.

The first line of each entry gives the tree's generic name only, printed in large capital letters: e.g., **PRUNUS** (the generic name for all apricots, cherries, peaches and plums, whether fruiting or ornamental).

The generic name is followed by one or more popular names; generally, these are the English names for the whole genus, or for its most prominent members. These are printed in normal type.

After this come three more lines in heavy type, each prefixed by an asterisk (*). The first line, e.g.,

* **Deciduous/fast**

indicates firstly whether the tree will drop all of its leaves at any one time or whether it is evergreen; a second group of words gives information about the tree's rate of growth to flowering maturity — fast, slow or medium.

The second line, e.g.,

* **Late spring/fragrant**

indicates the tree's principal season of floral display and whether or not the blooms are fragrant.

The third line, e.g.,

* **Ht: to 10m/30ft**

tells the tree's maximum height in metres and in feet and will help you decide where to plant it. Often the tree's height in cultivation will be only a fraction of its height in nature — if so, this will be indicated within the text. When more than one species of the particular tree genus is dealt with in the entry, this line will express the group's height as a range, e.g.,
Acacia:

* **Ht: 6-20m/18-60ft**

More information about height of individual species is given in the body of the text.

Finally, each heading includes a group of symbols (anywhere from 1 to 3). These are in the form of letters enclosed by a square.

C Shows that the tree grows well in cold-winter areas (though it may grow elsewhere in a shaded position).

T Shows that it thrives in any temperate climate (though its range may be wider).

H That the tree does best in a hot climate (tropical to subtropical). Very few tropical trees will flower in a cold winter climate.

As some trees are quite adaptable, however, the three squared symbols may appear in many different combinations.

Finally, at the right of each heading is a line drawing showing the tree's most common shape at maturity (or the shape of its most commonly raised species). These drawings can of necessity be only a very rough guide, except where only one species of the tree is both grown and described. Together with the tree's given height, they will enable you to calculate its probable spread.

Within the entry itself is all sorts of additional information for the home gardener or tree spotter. This includes country or range of origin; methods of propagation; soil requirements; natural pests; minimum winter temperature; ideal position or light intensity; uses in commerce, history and many other things. Generally, shape and appearance of foliage will be described, often with details of bark and fruit as well. There are also descriptions of popular colour varieties. Though each entry is necessarily brief, you'll find everything you need to know for raising and making best use of a whole world of wonderful flowering trees.

Acacia baileyana
Cootamundra Wattle

ACACIA

Wattle, Mimosa
* **Evergreen/fast**
* **Any season/ fragrant**
* **Ht: 6-20m/18-60ft** T H

Acacias seem so typically Australian that one of them (**A. pycnantha,** the Golden Wattle) has been adopted as the nation's floral symbol and wreaths the coat of arms. And yet they are by no means exclusive to the southern continent. Africa has nearly as many species, Asia and America quite a few, and Hawaii's native **A. koa** yields one of the finest of the world's timbers. There are about one thousand species throughout the world.

But Australia's **Acacias** are notably the most decorative, bursting into glowing masses of golden blossom at different times of the year according to species, but mostly in winter and spring. Viewing the dense puffball blossom for the first time, it comes as something of a surprise to learn that **Acacias** are very *un*typical members of the pea family, Leguminosae. But they do bear the same long pods as other peas, with the seeds attached alternately to either shell.

The leaves are quite a mixture. In fact most species do not bear leaves at all, merely *phyllodes* or stalks, which are generally flattened into a leaf-like shape, though in some species they may be adapted to a needle shape or even a spine. A few species, such as the lovely Cootamundra Wattle, **A. baileyana,** do bear true leaves in their adult state, and they are very delicate fern-like affairs. Each puffball 'flower' is actually a compact globular mass of many small flowers.

14 • FLOWERING TREES

Acacia terminalis
Cedar Wattle

ACACIA (continued)

Acacia blossom is generally sold as 'Mimosa' in Europe and America (where the cultivated plants were imported from Australia) but the true Mimosa is an entirely different, though related, plant. In Australia **Acacia** has always been known as Wattle, because the thin branches and trunks were often woven and then sealed with clay or mud to form walls of the earliest colonial houses. This form of construction was known in Europe as 'wattle and daub', but in Australia the name became attached to the plant.

Few Wattle species grow into large trees, or live very long. They do grow quickly, however, and are often used to provide quick colour in the new garden, or for protection from sun along fields and roads.

Acacia may be readily grown from seed, which should be heat-treated, either in boiling water or close to a fire, to split the tough casing. Some leaf-colour varieties are propagated from cuttings.

Many of the smaller **Acacia** species make useful stock fodder in times of drought, to which they are well adapted.

Acacia glaucescens
Coast Myall

Acacia decurrens
Black Wattle

Acacia longifolia
Sydney Golden Wattle ▶

A.15

Aesculus hippocastanum
Horse Chestnut

AESCULUS

Horse Chestnut
* **Deciduous/fast**
* **Spring/fragrant**
* **Ht: 10-35m/30-100ft**

Grown purely for aesthetic appeal, the spectacular **Aesculus** or Horse Chestnuts have no useful commercial qualities at all, and yet they have become possibly the most beloved of trees in cooler parts of the Northern Hemisphere for parks, street planting and large gardens.

Easily grown from seed or grafted cuttings of named colour varieties, the small number of **Aesculus** species are native to various parts of Europe, North America and Asia — **Aesculus** is the original Roman name.

The most handsome and most commonly seen is **A. hippocastanum,** a tall, long-lived tree found originally in the Balkans, and imported to England in the seventeenth century. Deciduous, it grows fast and may ultimately reach 30m in height, its striking, hand-shaped leaves being among the first to open in spring. These are followed by tall candles of white flowers later in the season; and in turn by round spiny fruits about the size of a golf ball. In a dry year, the leaves become badly scorched about the edges, but normally they turn a clear yellow in autumn. **A. hippocastanum** has become naturalized all over Europe and much of North America, and is also grown in cool climates of the Southern Hemisphere.

It has a pink-flowered hybrid, **A. X carnea.**

AGONIS

Willow Myrtle, Peppermint
* **Evergreen/slow**
* **Spring-summer/ fragrant**
* **Ht: to 12m/36ft**

|C| |T|

Light and delicate members of the Myrtle family (Eucalypts and Paperbarks are others), Western Australia's small group of **Agonis** species have found favour as an evergreen, dry-climate replacement for more delicate and deciduous willows. They are now seen as both garden specimens and street trees in southern Europe, South Africa, California and many other areas.

New plants may be propagated from seeds in spring, or from tip-cuttings taken in summer.

A. flexuosa, the Willow Myrtle or Peppermint tree, is most commonly seen. It may reach 12m in height, but is more usually a wide-spreading dwarf around shrub size. The foliage of the weeping branches is grey-green and willow-like, exudes a spicy peppermint odour when bruised. The flowers resemble those of **Leptospermum.**

Agonis flexuosa
Willow Myrtle

ALBERTA

(No popular name)
* **Evergreen/slow**
* **Early spring**
* **Ht: to 10m/30ft**

|T|
|H|

A small South African tree, sometimes not much above shrub size, **Alberta magna** was named for the famous thirteenth century philosopher, Albertus Magnus. Botanically it is classed in the family Rubiaceae, which also includes other subtropical favourites such as Gardenia, Luculia and Rondeletia. The foliage consists of glossy 15cm leaves that are handsome all year, while the flower display (generally in winter or early spring) appears in terminal panicles. These consist of a number of scarlet, 5-petalled tubular blossoms which look quite stunning against the background of dark foliage. Each bloom is about 2.5cm in length, and is followed by a small fruit encased in two enlarged calyx lobes.

Alberta may be grown from seed or cuttings.

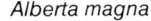

Alberta magna

Albizzia julibrissin
Persian Silk Tree

ALBIZZIA

Silk Tree, Cape Wattle
* **Deciduous/fast**
* **Spring-summer**
* **Ht: 10-25m/30-75ft**

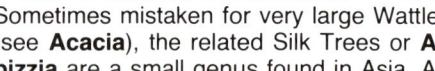

Sometimes mistaken for very large Wattles (see **Acacia**), the related Silk Trees or **Albizzia** are a small genus found in Asia, Africa and Australia, with one unimportant species in Mexico.

Most commonly planted is the large **A. lebbek** or Siris Tree, a 25m favourite for shade and shelter throughout the subtropical regions of the world. It bears deciduous bipinnate leaves like a Jacaranda, uninteresting panicles of greenish wattle-flowers for a few days in late spring, and then an absolute mass of brown pods. These are the tree's main display as they move and chatter ceaselessly in the wind. In the Philippines, they call it the Woman's Tongue tree!

The Australian species **A. lophantha** or Cape Wattle grows only half the size, often with a shrubby habit. Again, its leaves are bipinnate, though rather larger, and its petal-less flowers are greenish, forming bottlebrush-style spikes in the leaf axils.

Prettiest of the genus is the Persian Silk Tree, **A. julibrissin,** a favourite in the Middle East, Australia, France, California and many other temperate climates. It is a short, spreading tree decked lavishly in summer with large clusters of pink puffball flowers at branch ends. It has several cultivars with deeper coloured flowers and is

ALBIZZIA (continued)

quite hardy down to −12°C/10°F.

The Ceylon Rosewood, **A. odoratissima,** also grows to 25m, and has coarse, bipinnate leaves. The yellowish flowers appear in sparse, 30cm spikes. Its fragrant timber is used for cabinet work.

The timber of **A. lebbek** is also much sought after for cabinet work, being heavy and beautifully figured. The bark of all species is powdered and used as soap in many primitive societies, and the leaves and seed pods are used as cattle fodder.

Albizzias were named for an Italian naturalist, Albizzi, and are readily propagated from seed.

Albizzia lophantha
Cape Wattle

ALECTRYON

Native Quince, Titoki
* **Evergreen/fast**
* **Summer**
* **Ht: 10m/30ft**

A small but useful genus of trees scattered throughout the Pacific from Australia to Hawaii, **Alectryon** has only two species in general cultivation, **A. excelsa,** the Titoki from New Zealand, and **A. subcinereus,** the Native Quince from eastern Australia, both resembling the European Ash trees.

Alectryons are slender trees rarely exceeding 10m in height and with pinnate leaves. The Titoki can be recognized from its black bark, 45cm leaves which have one leaflet more on one side of the leaf-stem, and creamy flowers. Its tough timber is valued for cabinet making and wooden tool-handles.

The Australian Native Quince, **A. subcinereus,** has grey bark and smaller pinnate leaves without a terminal leaflet. The flower clusters are short and followed by smooth berries borne in pairs, each with one seed in a red, fleshy surround.

Alectryon is propagated from seed, and is related to the popular Asian fruit Rambutan **(Nephelium lappaceum).**

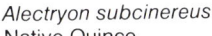
Alectryon subcinereus
Native Quince

Aleurites moluccana
Candlenut, Kukui

Amherstia nobilis
Pride of Burma

ALEURITES

Candlenut, Kukui
* **Evergreen/fast** [T]
* **All year**
* **Ht: to 20m/60ft** [H]

The striking Candlenut tree, **Aleurites moluccana,** is found in hillside forests of the Pacific Islands and South-East Asia. It is one of the great domesticated trees of the world, with a thousand uses, and has been adopted as the official tree emblem of Hawaii.

The Candlenut may reach 20m in height and is densely clothed with three- or five-lobed leaves, pale green, with a rusty fuzz on the undersides. The tiny white flowers are borne several times a year, followed by clusters of 5cm nuts.

Several closely related species are grown for their commercial value. They include the Japan Wood-oil Tree, **A. cordata,** the Tung-oil Tree, **A. fordii** and the Mu-oil Tree, **A. montana.**

All may be grown from seed or cuttings, and are found in gardens around the world.

AMHERSTIA

Pride of Burma
* **Evergreen/fast**
* **Summer**
* **Ht: to 13m/40ft** [H]

The gorgeous **Amherstia nobilis,** only one of its genus, has been hailed as the most beautiful flowering tree in the world. Simple, light, lacy, it grows to 13m in the wild.

The graceful 1m leaves have six or eight pairs of leaflets, and new growth (like that of some other tropical trees very flaccid and colourful) is often shaded with bronze, red and purple. The flower clusters hang from the branches like inverted candelabra. Individual blossoms remind some people of orchids, others of hummingbirds. They are pale pink, spotted and marked in red and white, with a splash of golden yellow on the large upper petal.

Amherstias are generally propagated from cuttings and have flowered in Hawaii, the Philippines, Florida, the Caribbean, South America and even in England, under glass.

Angophora costata
Apple Gum

ANGOPHORA

Apple Gum
* **Evergreen/fast**
* **Summer**
* **Ht: to 27m/80ft**

The **Angophoras** or Apple Gums are a very small Australian genus greatly resembling the Eucalypts. They have achieved world popularity in other dry areas such as California and South Africa, but they are native to the fast-draining sandstone of the east coast of Australia.

They have elegant orange or pinkish bark, which peels unevenly from the trunk, and two forms of leaf — pale green, heart-shaped juvenile foliage and long drooping adult leaves up to 12.5cm long. The flowers (invariably cream) are very largely a mass of stamens, but unlike the Eucalypts, they also have small petals. The fruits that follow are like gumnuts, but ribbed. With all their decorative qualities, the **Angophoras** have escaped annihilation in Australia because the timber is not of much use except for firewood.

Only two species are commonly planted, the tall and graceful **A. costata** or Smooth-barked Apple Gum, and the smaller **A. cordifolia** or Dwarf Apple Gum, which has a rugged spreading appearance and rarely exceeds 4m in height.

The taller **Angophora floribunda** or Gum Myrtle is found further inland, thrives in sandy soil and has a noticeably rough bark.

Arbutus unedo
Irish Strawberry

ARBUTUS

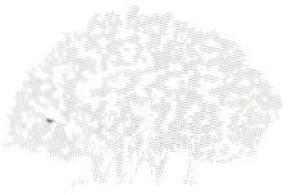

Irish Strawberry, Madrone
* **Evergreen/medium**
* **Autumn-spring/fragrant**
* **Ht: 10-30m/30-100ft**

The name Irish Strawberry must be a hangover from some earlier Irish joke. Birds and bugs and children playing games are likely to appreciate the fruit, but hardly anyone else.

But the tree itself is another matter! Seek **Arbutus unedo** out in autumn when the branches are almost weighed down with tiny, fragrant flowers, drooping just like lily of the valley.

Arbutus is an old Latin name, and the tree has beautifully gnarled, reddish branches and shiny, serrated, elliptical leaves. The flowers are white or pink.

At the other end of Europe grows the very similar but taller **A. andrachne** of Greece and Asia Minor, with the flowers borne in erect spikes.

Half a world away, in California, is **A. menziesii,** the Madrone or California Strawberry Tree. It is tallest of all, reaching 30m. Its decorative terracotta bark peels away in large flaky patches, and the pink flowers appear in spring.

Somewhere in between the European and North American species is **A. canariensis** from the Canary Islands. Its leaves are softer in texture, the flowers green and pink.

AZARA

(No popular name)
* **Evergreen/slow**
* **Late spring/fragrant**
* **Ht: to 5m/15ft**

Azaras are small trees or shrubs from Chile, bearing tiny golden flowers that have a rich chocolatey perfume out of all proportion to their size. Several species are grown in sheltered areas of temperate gardens; all enjoy protection from strong sun, and well-drained soil. Ample water and regular feeding are necessary to turn on a good blossom display. The ovate leaves of **Azara dentata** are finely toothed and glossy above, slightly hairy on the reverse and 2.5cm in width. The tree develops a rounded shape and branches densely; can be pruned to a useful hedge. The small clusters of fluffy blossom are at their best in late spring. Related **A. lanceolata** blooms earlier, has larger 6cm leaves.

Azara dentata

BACKHOUSIA

Lemon-scented Myrtle,
Sweet Verbena Tree
* **Evergreen/fast**
* **Summer/fragrant**
* **Ht: 8m/24ft**

Looking for a tree that's really lemon-charged? You don't need to go beyond **Backhousia citriodora,** a slim, neat specimen rarely passing 8m. It has attracted many common names, not only in its native Australia, but also in South Africa, USA and Europe: Sweet Verbena Tree, and Lemon-scented Myrtle among them.

It is easily raised from half-ripe cuttings taken in spring, grows fast in rich acid soil. **Backhousia** is deservedly popular, not only for its handsome leaves with strong citrus fragrance, but also for the clouds of tiny four-petalled white flowers produced in early summer. These soon fall but are outlived by the tiny green calyces, which are the tree's principal display.

B. citriodora is also raised commercially, the foliage being crushed for a citrus-scented oil.

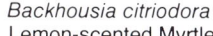

Backhousia citriodora
Lemon-scented Myrtle

Banksia integrifolia
Coastal Banksia

Banksia grandis
Bull Banksia

BANKSIA

Banksia, Honeysuckle
* **Evergreen/slow**
* **Winter/Summer**
* **Ht: 5-13m/15-40ft** C   T

There is no written proof that Sir Joseph Banks chose this genus to be his namesake. But he was known to be immensely proud of his discovery of these curious trees, that first day ashore at Botany Bay, in April 1770.

At any rate it was named **Banksia serrata,** the Red Honeysuckle, only the first of many related species found in succeeding years. The Red Honeysuckle is still a feature of the Australian east coast vegetation from Tasmania to Queensland, its gnarled trunk twisting into picturesque shapes among the outcrops of sandstone.

The bark is brown and deeply furrowed, covering a striking blood-red timber. The leathery leaflets are sharply toothed. But **Banksia** flowerheads are the most interesting feature, stunning 15cm spikes of tubular golden flowers arranged in neat parallel rows. As these gradually open from the base upwards, the entire inflorescence takes on a fuzzy appearance as the wiry stamens emerge one by one. **Banksia** flowers are notably rich in nectar, and the popular name of Honeysuckle is in reference to their attraction for birds and insects. As the flowers fall, the woody stalk takes on a bizarre appearance as individual seed cells open like a series of gaping mouths. Children call these 'Banksia Men', and Australian author May Gibbs based a series of nightmarish figures on them in her children's stories.

Banksias are most useful trees in poor sandy coastal soil, being completely salt-resistant. The closely related Coastal Banksia **(B. integrifolia)** bears inflorescences of a greenish yellow tone; its leaves are smooth-edged with silver reverses, the trunk smooth and deep grey.

The majority of **Banksia** species are classed as shrubs, but there are several more of tree size, with spectacular flowers. They include the orange **B. ericifolia** or Heath-leaf Banksia, the silver and orange **B. menziesii** and yellow **B. grandis.**

Banksia ericifolia
Heath-leaf Banksia ▶

B.25

BARKLYA

Gold Blossom Tree
* **Evergreen**/slow   T
* **Summer**
* **Ht: to 20m/60ft**   H

There is very little about the **Barklya** to suggest at a distance that it is a member of the pea family Leguminosae, not even the tell-tale long pods. But that's what it is — a handsome but uncommon member of the rainforest flora in New South Wales and Queensland, named for a forgotten British Colonial Governor. It is a magnificent tree, the only one of its genus, and easily propagated from seed or cuttings, if you can beg, borrow or steal some.

B. syringifolia may reach 20m in a warm sunny position. As its specific name suggests, its leaves are heart-shaped, exactly like those of lilacs **(Syringa)**. The vivid orange-yellow pea flowers appear in long, stiff spikes in early summer, in superb contrast to the dark trunk and foliage. They are followed by small 5cm pods with one or two seeds each.

Barklya seems to be able to withstand temperatures down to −2°C/28°F and has been raised in France, South Africa and Hawaii, though not apparently on the mainland of the United States.

Not commonly stocked by nurserymen, **Barklya** is worth seeking out for one of the most spectacular displays in the summer garden.

Barklya syringifolia
Gold Blossom Tree

Bauhinia monandra
St Thomas' Tree

BAUHINIA

Orchid Tree,
St Thomas' Tree
* **Deciduous/fast**
* **Winter-spring**
* **Ht: 7-17m/20-50ft**

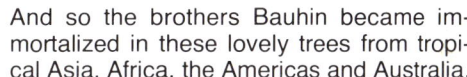

In the eighteenth century, when a new tree genus was discovered that bore uniquely twin-lobed leaves, a suitably paired name was soon forthcoming. **Bauhinia!** A diligent search had revealed the names of two sixteenth century botanists, twins perhaps, brothers certainly. And so the brothers Bauhin became immortalized in these lovely trees from tropical Asia, Africa, the Americas and Australia.

Most **Bauhinias** grow readily from cuttings or seed, will thrive in any climate down to a winter minimum of 7°C/45°F. The species most commonly grown is **B. variegata,** the Mountain Ebony from India, a slight, graceful plant, rarely surpassing a height of 7m. It is cultivated worldwide for the sheer beauty of its floral display — wonderful mauve-pink blossoms with five overlapped petals often variegated in pink or purple.

Its smaller variety **B. variegata alba** (the

28 • FLOWERING TREES

Bauhinia variegata alba
White Orchid Tree

Bauhinia blakeana
Hong Kong Orchid Tree

BAUHINIA (continued)

White Orchid Tree) bears flowers of purest white and lime green. Both flower in early spring and better after a cold winter, when the deciduous leaves drop early.

Chinese **B. purpurea** is similar in habit, but flowers more in the purple range, its petals larger and quite separate. **B. monandra** is tropical. Its blooms open white, marked in red and yellow, the whole rapidly changing to a rich pink.

The Hong Kong Orchid Tree, **B. blakeana,** is the floral symbol of that small colony, an evergreen sterile hybrid that bears splashy reddish-purple flowers in autumn and winter. Australian **B. hookeri,** a 12m tree from tropical Queensland, has now been rechristened **Lysiphyllum.**

Apart from the Australian species, most Orchid Trees need vigorous pruning to develop a recognizably tree-like shape.

As tree members of the pea family, all **Bauhinias** bear long bean-like pods which frequently turn brown and hang on the tree in an unsightly fashion until the new foliage appears.

Bauhinia variegata
Mountain Ebony

Bixa orellana
Lipstick Tree

BIXA

Lipstick Tree, Annatto
* **Evergreen/fast**
* **Summer**
* **Ht: 10m/30ft**

Grown as an ornamental in warm climate gardens everywhere, the Lipstick Tree, **Bixa orellana,** is native to the Amazon region. Grown easily and quickly from seed or cuttings, it is inclined to be bushy in shape.

Bixa may reach 10m in warm climates, and the evergreen heart-shaped leaves may be 18cm in length. All summer long, charming pink and white flowers, like single wild roses, appear at the tips of branches, and these are succeeded by clusters of almond-shaped red-brown fruit covered in soft spines.

In the days before synthetics revolutionized industry, the tree was planted commercially for dye used to colour cheese, margarine, chocolate, fabric, paints — and, of course, lipstick, hence the popular name.

Bombax ellipticum
Shaving Brush Tree

Bombax malabaricum
Red Silk Cotton

BOMBAX

Silk Cotton, Barrigon, Shaving Brush Tree
* **Deciduous/fast**
* **Spring**
* **Ht: 15-35m/45-100ft**

From tropical forests of Asia, South America and Africa comes a genus of splendid specimen trees called **Bombax**. Their rather jingoistic name is in fact an ancient Greek word for cotton, although the filaments obtained from their bulky seed pods are far too fine to spin, and are used instead as a substitute for kapok.

B. malabaricum, the Red Silk Cotton Tree from South-East Asia, is the most commonly seen species, in gardens of northern Australia, Hong Kong, Africa, Hawaii and many other places. It is a tall tree, reaching 35m and more, with a widely buttressed trunk at maturity. Easily raised from seed, this **Bombax** needs deep soil and lots of moisture all year round to grow really well and produce its stunning crop of 18cm red flowers in early spring. These appear at the ends of branches shortly after the tree loses its foliage for a brief period in winter.

Bombax leaves are strikingly hand-shaped and up to 50cm across, consisting of three to seven widely spread leaflets. The trunk is sometimes spiny, and the tree may need a little pruning and staking when young to force a tidy pyramidal shape.

The Shaving-brush Tree, **B. ellipticum,** is smaller all round. The height is unlikely to pass 25m, the leaves are 45cm wide with five leaflets, coppery-red when young. Flowers (to 25cm long) consist of five purplish-red petals which curl back to reveal a mass of white stamens in spring. The 10cm pods are full of a greenish fibre, and the bark is patterned in a magnificent snake-skin effect of blurred grey and green.

The Barrigon, **B. barrigon** is a much smaller tree, rarely reaching 15m in height. The leaves, with 7-9 leaflets, are only 30cm in diameter, while the flowers are white and many-stamened. The heavy trunk has a strongly buttressed appearance.

In gardens of north Australia one finds **B. ceiba,** a sprawling, spiny tree with flowers more brilliant than **B. malabaricum.**

Brachychiton acerifolium
Illawarra Flame

BRACHYCHITON

Kurrajong, Lacebark,
Illawarra Flame
* **Deciduous/slow**
* **Spring-summer**
* **Ht: 10-35m/30-100 ft**

Considered by many to be Australia's most spectacular genus of flowering trees, the Kurrajongs (**Brachychiton** spp.) are maddeningly irregular in their flowering habits. But in a good early summer, a garden specimen of the Illawarra Flame (**B. acerifolium**) is a sight never to be forgotten — a vivid scarlet blur! The effect is heightened if it is contrasted with the mauve flowers of a nearby Jacaranda, which blooms at the same time.

The **Brachychitons** are most variable in size, in shape of trunk and leaves, and in size and colouring of flowers, which are generally bell-shaped. Those native to the semitropical forests of Australia's moist east coast tend to grow tall and flower profusely on the bare tree after leaf fall, in summer. Others, native to the dry Australian outback, are generally smaller in size with bloated water-storing trunks. Their flowers are less showy and tend to appear

32 • FLOWERING TREES

Brachychiton discolor
Queensland Lacebark

BRACHYCHITON (continued)

under the new summer foliage which is used for fodder in drought-stricken areas.

A peculiarity of the Kurrajongs is the extreme leaf variation. On one tree of **B. populneum,** for instance, you may find simple pointed leaves, rather like poplar foliage, and others that are long and divided into anything from three to nine pointed lobes. Because of this, it is sometimes listed as **B. diversifolia,** though there is no true species of this name.

All the Kurrajongs thrive in warm, dryish climates such as California, South Africa and the Mediterranean, but the desert species do not do well in the moister subtropics like Hawaii and Hong Kong.

Wood of many Kurrajong species has been used in the Australian outback for shingles and fencing, but generally they are cultivated only for their decorative and shade-giving qualities.

The name **Brachychiton** is of Greek origin. There are many intermediate hybrids, and all can be grown from seed or cuttings.

Brachychiton populneum
Kurrajong

Brachychiton populneo-acerifolium
Pink Kurrajong

Brassaia actinophylla
Octopus Tree

BRASSAIA

Queensland Umbrella Tree, Octopus Tree
* **Evergreen/fast**
* **Spring-summer**
* **Ht: to 13m/40ft**

Propagated everywhere by the thousand, as one of the world's top ten indoor plants, Queensland's **Brassaia actinophylla** or Octopus Tree gives no hint of its full potential until you've seen it growing unrestrained in a subtropical garden.

The handsome, umbrella-shaped compound leaves are still there, but are 1m in diameter and borne all over a many-branched tree up to 13m in height. And throughout spring and summer an extraordinary floral phenomenon appears from the heart of each leaf cluster — a series of curved and twisting flower stems looking exactly like the tentacles of a red octopus. These appear to be covered on one side with round sucker shapes, which close inspection reveals to be the heads of small red flowers, followed by purplish fruit.

Brassaia can be raised from quite large cuttings or air-layers.

The Octopus Tree enjoys warmth and plenty of water, and its normal habit is to form a single trunk with almost vertical branches appearing from quite low down. If you prefer a denser, more bushy plant, just keep cutting it back.

Brassaia is still often listed incorrectly as a **Schefflera,** which is a related genus (see **Schefflera**).

Brownea grandiceps
Rose of Venezuela

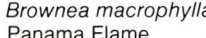

Brownea macrophylla
Panama Flame

BROWNEA

Rose of Venezuela, Panama Flame

* **Evergreen or deciduous/fast**
* **Spring**
* **Ht: 10-20m/30-60ft**

The huge, cabbage-sized, orange-red flower clusters of this wonderful South American tree, **Brownea grandiceps,** the Rose of Venezuela, almost play hide-and-seek among its dense foliage. Look more closely and you will notice that each head is composed of dozens of tubular, reddish blossoms with yellow stamens, fitted together like a hatmaker's tulle confection.

B. grandiceps like others of its genus was named for Patrick Brown, an Irish-born author and physician of Jamaica. It is a tall tree, growing up to 20m in its jungle home, but of course not so high in cultivation. The trunk is stout, the branches greyish and woolly to the touch, and the foliage consists of great rosettes of compound leaves, each up to 1m in length and consisting of about twelve pairs of large leaflets. The young foliage is flaccid and usually highly coloured, and the tree is generally evergreen in a tropical climate.

Even more spectacular in the warm climate garden is the smaller Panama Flame, **B. macrophylla.** The flowers of this species are inclined to open before the deciduous foliage and are a brilliant mass of gold, pink and scarlet long-stemmed blossoms that pop directly out of the slender trunk and branches. Individual flower masses may be 1m in circumference on older trees. It has woolly brown branches and compound leaves of six to twelve leaflets, each about 35cm in length. This tree is very variable in shape, but usually columnar, with a light, open habit.

Several other **Browneas** are in cultivation, all suited to the warm-climate, frost-free garden. These include **B. capitella,** a Venezuelan species with 27cm orange flower heads; and **B. coccinea,** the Scarlet Flame Bean, a low, spreading tree with weeping branches. It produces 20cm compound leaves with 2-5 pairs of leaflets and a profuse crop of small, scarlet pea-flowers borne in clusters directly from older branches.

Brugmansia suaveolens
Angel's Trumpets

Brugmansia sanguinea
Red Datura

BRUGMANSIA
(syn DATURA)

Angel's Trumpets, Datura
* **Evergreen/very fast**
* **Summer/very fragrant**
* **Ht: 3-6m/10-20ft**

A superb genus of flowering trees from cool areas of South America, the **Brugmansias** (often sold as **Datura**) need wind protection for they are inclined to be top-heavy. They have 30cm leaves and fragrant trumpet flowers to 25cm in length, resembling related petunias. They grow in almost any climate short of hard-frost areas — a mild frost will render them unsightly, but they'll soon recover when warm weather returns. **B. suaveolens** and **B. candida** are similar, bearing enormous white trumpet flowers in summer and autumn — these are deliciously fragrant at night. Smaller **B. sanguinea** has gorgeous orange-red trumpets. All are attractive to caterpillars and other chewing pests because of the plants' narcotic content.

Buckinghamia celsissima
Ivory Curl Tree

BUCKINGHAMIA

Ivory Curl Tree
* **Evergreen/slow**
* **Late summer**
* **Ht: 6-20m/20-60ft**

A profusely flowering tree from the rainforests of southern Queensland, **Buckinghamia** has proved amenable to cultivation over quite a wide climatic range, though its size is directly related to the amount of year-round heat it gets. It has flowered successfully in areas where the temperature drops to freezing point.

Like so many of Australia's other flowering trees it is a member of the Proteaceae family, and there is only one species. This may reach 20m in a suitably warm climate, but rarely passes 6m in cultivation.

The glossy, leathery leaves closely resemble those of the related **Macadamia** (which see). They are evergreen and greyish beneath. The flowers, borne in late summer, are up to 22cm long, consist of long spikes of curled creamy florets, reminiscent of ostrich plumes. As the florets open, the flower spikes weep under their own weight until the entire tree is a mass of fragrant blossom. Bees naturally adore it.

B. celsissima has been used successfully as a street tree in Queensland and New South Wales, and should do equally well in South Africa and the southern United States. It is best raised from seed.

BUTEA

Flame of the Forest,
Pulas, Dhak Tree
* **Deciduous/slow**
* **Spring**
* **Ht: to 16m/50ft** T H

A brilliantly flowering specimen tree for the warm-climate garden, the **Butea** or Dhak Tree will tolerate a wider range of soil conditions than many of its semitropical relatives.

It is a slow-growing, rather gnarled tree of stark appearance until the flowers burst open in spring. These are arranged as 15cm racemes of curved, orange-red pea flowers with a marvellous silvery sheen. They are followed by long pea pods which are grey and furry. The foliage consists of a number of 20cm compound leaves, each made up of three leaflets, blue-green in colour.

In its native Bangladesh and Burma, the **Butea** is known also as the Pulas Tree and Flame of the Forest. The sap is valued locally as an astringent, and the entire tree yields a gum known as Bengal Kino. The flowers are often distilled into an orange dye.

A splendid choice for warm coastal gardens, **B. frondosa** will resist a degree of salt. It is also suited to saline desert soils and will even put up with an occasional light frost.

Butea frondosa
Dhak Tree

Caesalpinia pulcherrima
Barbadoes Pride

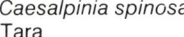
Caesalpinia spinosa
Tara

CAESALPINIA

Barbadoes Pride, Tara, Dwarf Poinciana, Leopard Tree, Brazilwood
* **Semi-deciduous/fast**
* **Warm weather**
* **Ht: 5-17m/15-50ft** [T] [H]

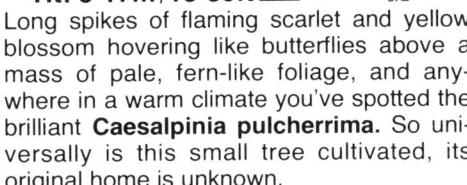

Long spikes of flaming scarlet and yellow blossom hovering like butterflies above a mass of pale, fern-like foliage, and anywhere in a warm climate you've spotted the brilliant **Caesalpinia pulcherrima.** So universally is this small tree cultivated, its original home is unknown.

It grows readily from seed, rarely reaching more than 4m, and the foliage is so dense it is sometimes trimmed to hedge height and known as Barbadoes Flower Fence. What a sight it makes with gorgeous flower spikes appearing all along its length — scarlet and yellow, plain orange or pink.

Long stamens and the flat green pods of the pea family are other points of identification on this spiky-branched sapling, the commonest, but by no means the only one, of a dazzling tropical genus. There are about 35 species altogether.

Next in popularity would probably be the Leopard Tree, **C. ferrea.** This grows fast to 17m, and flowers in late summer, the brilliant yellow blossoms appearing like a golden haze above a feathery crown that lets through plenty of light. Its special beauty is in the bark, a smooth surface shaded in beige, grey and white, constantly changing pattern as the flakes peel. The leaves are compound, with up to 64 broad leaflets.

A rather similar tree is the Brazilwood, **C. echinata,** which has a spiny trunk and is the national tree of Brazil. It grows to 10m, and the compound leaves have diamond-shaped leaflets. The flowers are yellow and long-stamened.

C. spinosa, the Tara, has red-margined yellow blooms, grows to 7m.

Most **Caesalpinias** are native to Central and South America, although there are representatives in India, Japan, Africa, China and northern Australia. The pods and bark of many are sought commercially for tannin and dye, while the Malaysian Sappanwood, **C. sappan,** is the source of a valuable commercial timber.

Callicoma serratifolia
Blackwattle

CALLICOMA

Blackwattle
* **Evergreen/fast**
* **Spring**
* **Ht: to 10m/30ft** C T

From the appearance of its fluffy cream flower-clusters, it is easy to see why this tree also was given the name 'wattle' in Australia's early colonial times. They certainly do resemble the flowers of **Acacia** but in fact belong to quite a different family, the Saxifragaceae.

At one time, **Callicomas** grew densely around Sydney Harbour, but have virtually disappeared with the spread of suburbia, because they enjoy shaded places and the shelter of other trees.

The 15cm serrated leaves, long-oval in shape, are a pleasant, light green when young. The Blackwattle ranges from shrub size to 10m in height. It is shallow-rooted, enjoys the same acid soils and humid conditions as Azaleas, Rhododendrons and Camellias, but grows over a much wider climatic range and is a popular garden specimen in many countries away from its native continent.

The name **Callicoma** roughly translates as 'beautiful hair', a reference to the profuse golden stamens.

C. serratifolia, the name of the grown species, merely means that it has serrated leaves.

FLOWERING TREES

Callistemon salignus
Willow Bottlebrush

CALLISTEMON

Bottlebrush   [C]
* **Evergreen**/fast   [T]
* **Spring**
* **Ht: 7-13m/20-40ft**

Like much of the natural Australian vegetation, the colourful genus **Callistemon** is part of the Myrtle family, as are **Angophora, Backhousia, Eucalyptus, Leptospermum, Melaleuca** and **Syzygium,** to list only a few of the trees represented elsewhere in this book.

But the special glory of **Callistemons** is their long spikes of flowers without petals, just a mass of clustered stamens arranged in formal rows, like a bottlebrush. The name **Callistemon** is in fact Greek for 'beautiful stamens'. These bottlebrushes appear

Callistemon viminalis
Weeping Bottlebrush

Callistemon shiressii
Cream Bottlebrush

Callistemon citrinus
Crimson Bottlebrush

CALLISTEMON (continued)

profusely in many shades of crimson and scarlet, in cream and white, and even in pink, green or violet in less-common species.

The Weeping Bottlebrush, **C. viminalis,** in particular, has become a much sought-after garden specimen in Florida, California and Hawaii, in southern England, South Africa, Hong Kong and the Mediterranean area. Like most other **Callistemons** it is found naturally in low-lying ground or even creek beds, which makes it particularly useful for badly drained sites, or for planting on the low side of built-up roads and driveways.

A fast grower with a graceful willow-like habit, it may reach 5m in five or six years, and the maximum flower display is in late spring.

Another species of similar habit is the White or Willow Bottlebrush, **C. salignus.** This is perhaps a little sturdier, resisting a degree or two of frost, and quite amenable to the salt spray of coastal gardens. The bottlebrushes, borne at the ends of weeping branchlets, are pale cream and contrast beautifully with the rosy pink of new foliage.

A third common species is **C. citrinus,** which bears crimson flowers. Its foliage is distinctively lemon-scented, the new leaves a soft pink.

Bottlebrushes are generally propagated from cuttings.

Calodendron capense
Cape Chestnut

CALODENDRON

Cape Chestnut
* **Evergreen/fast**
* **Spring-summer/fragrant**
* **Ht: to 20m/60ft**

One of Africa's most delightful trees, heavily flowering **Calodendron capense** or Cape Chestnuts are now seen in gardens all over the temperate to tropical world: they even resist winter temperatures as low as −5°C/22°F.

Best propagated from cuttings, it will grow rapidly to 7m and more slowly thereafter, particularly in cooler areas. The handsomely spotted leaves are evergreen in warm climates, but may be deciduous elsewhere. It will usually flower in either late summer or early spring, but more rarely at other times of the year, according to the individual tree.

The 10cm flowers, which appear in open spikes at branch ends, each have five curling pink petals, five crimson-spotted petaloids and five rigid pink stamens. They are highly perfumed, pick well, and are reminiscent of Rhododendron blooms.

Calodendrons like water at all times, and are not for dry areas. They prefer the company and shelter of other trees, when they will grow to taller and more striking specimens. When exposed they tend to grow too horizontal and may fall over in a heavy wind.

CAMELLIA C

Chinese Rose, Japonica, Sasanqua
* **Evergreen**/slow T
* **Autumn-spring flowers**
* **Ht: to 7m/21ft**

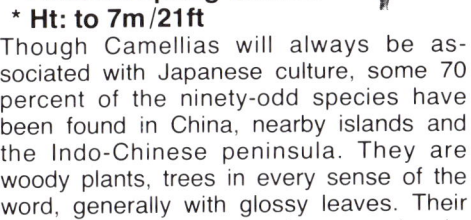

Though Camellias will always be associated with Japanese culture, some 70 percent of the ninety-odd species have been found in China, nearby islands and the Indo-Chinese peninsula. They are woody plants, trees in every sense of the word, generally with glossy leaves. Their usual habitat is mountainous and subtropical, where they grow in partial shade.

The flowers of the vast majority of the genus **Camellia** are neither large nor spectacular, but less than 4cm in diameter and plain white. Even smaller are the blooms of the most widely cultivated **Camellia** species, **C. sinensis.** This is the plant we know as tea, found naturally over a wide range centring on Assam, where it has been known to reach 17m. Its small white blooms are rarely seen except in specialist collections, but in plantations of many tropical areas its new leaf buds are picked for the finest grades of tea, and all leaves may be used in inferior blends.

It is because of the tea plant that the West first learned that there were **Camellia** species actually grown for their flowers. Though the beverage had been drunk for uncounted centuries, and was closely associated with the Buddhist religion, it did not reach Europe until mid-17th century, and was immediately adopted by fashionable society. The British East India Company, sensing a commercial bonanza, tried to export some of the tea plants by bribing Chinese officials. But it seems the Chinese outsmarted the company and substituted plants of the more decorative **C. japonica,** the leaves of which were useless for tea making. These first plants of **C. japonica** arrived in England early in the 18th century, and their blooms immediately caught the fancy of nurserymen. Their rapid growth in popularity may be judged by the fact that the number of **Camellia** varieties bred since, from these few early plants, is estimated to be as high as 20,000!

Camellia japonica 'Lalla Rookh' ▶

Camellia japonica at Descanso Gardens

Camellia sasanqua 'Setsugekka'

CAMELLIA (continued)

Far and away the majority of ornamental **Camellias** are descended from the wild **C. japonica,** a rather scraggy looking tree of 15m found naturally in Japan, eastern China, and Korea. Today, its descendants look better, flower better, pruned to a more compact height and width.

Plants of all varieties prefer protection from full sun, a deep, neutral to slightly acid soil. Reproduce their natural forest surroundings of shade, good drainage and humidity, and you can't go wrong! **Camellias** are grown in almost all coastal areas of Australia, in New Zealand, the western and south-eastern states of the USA, and in parts of Europe warmed by the Gulf Stream and Mediterranean.

The third most widely cultivated species of **Camellia** is **C. sasanqua,** a slender, densely-foliaged 5m tree from southern Japan and nearby islands, where it was cultivated for the fine oil extracted from its fruits. Originally white-flowered, there is

Camellia reticulata 'Francie L'

CAMELLIA (continued)

now a wide range of colours; the blooms are smaller and often lightly fragrant, but they do not last well. It extends the **Camellia** season by several months. **Sasanquas** can take more sun than **japonicas.**

The fourth widely grown **Camellia** species is a relative newcomer, **C. reticulata,** found naturally in the forests of southern China at altitudes of 2000-3000 metres. It is an open-growing tree up to 16m in height, with large, heavily-veined leaves and pink blooms up to 9cm in diameter in the wild.

It was introduced to Western gardens only in the 1930s, and used largely in hybridization until the discovery in 1948 that gigantic **reticulata** cultivars had been grown in the southern Chinese province of Yunnan for centuries. Some of these plants were imported to the USA and elsewhere in 1948-49, and when they bloomed with flowers up to 15cm in diameter, the rest was botanical history. Now it is these enormous **C. reticulata** cultivars and their Western-bred hybrids that catch the eye at all Camellia shows. They have proved to be no more difficult to grow than the **japonicas** and **sasanquas,** and though their present range of colours is limited, hybridists are extending it with every year that passes.

Camptotheca acuminata

CAMPTOTHECA

(No popular name)
* **Deciduous/fast**
* **Late spring**
* **Ht: to 23m/75ft** ⊤

A relative of the beautiful Dove Tree, **Davidia** (which see), **Camptotheca acuminata** is also native to China, but not widely grown, possibly because of its size. It may grow to all of 23m in deep, rich, mountain soil, and develops wide-spreading, weeping branches. Its ovate, pointed leaves are handsome, deeply-veined and up to 15cm in length. They are completely deciduous. The curious flowers appear late spring, borne in hanging, long-stemmed clusters, and looking rather like a pincushion with long white stamens projecting quite a distance from each 5-petalled, greenish-white flower. These are followed by shining brown samaras or fruits, each contained in a fallen flower's five-lobed calyx. They need plenty of water, particularly when flowers are developing.

CANANGA

Ylang Ylang, Perfume Tree
* **Evergreen**/fast
* **Autumn**/fragrant
* **Ht: to 25m/80ft**

Even the poor-sighted could hardly overlook **Cananga odorata** planted nearby, for its appeal is as much to the nose as to the eye. It is unfortunately purely a tree for the warmer climate, found naturally over a wide area from Burma down through Malaysia and Indonesia to the north of Australia.

A tall, rather narrow tree, with weeping, brittle branches, it bears long, rippled, compound leaves. In the axils, in autumn, appear clusters of the most striking, long-lasting flowers. They are up to 7.5cm across, with five thin, drooping petals. These are lime green at first, ripening to a warm orange after a few days, and are overpoweringly fragrant, particularly in the early morning.

In parts of its native range, **Cananga** is also known as the Perfume Tree or Ylang Ylang (which means the same thing), and individual blossoms are worn about the person or placed in cupboards to perfume linen. Earlier this century, they were used to scent coconut oil for a hairdressing which was sold as Macassar oil.

They are widely planted in Hawaii, but not often seen in their native Australia, which is a pity.

Cananga odorata
Ylang Ylang

CAPPARIS

Caper Tree, Cat's Whisker
* **Evergreen/fast**
* **Summer/fragrant**
* **Ht: to 5m/15ft**

[H]

A most variable genus, 300-odd species of Caper or **Capparis** are found in subtropical or tropical areas of both the new and old worlds. They include herbs, shrubs, trees and climbers, often with exquisite flowers. Shrubby Mediterranean species **C. spinosa** is raised commercially, and its pickled flower buds are the tangy capers with many culinary uses. But here, we are concerned with the tree species.

The Jamaica Caper Tree, **C. cynophallophora,** is popularly grown in the Caribbean and southern USA. It bears leathery, elliptical 10cm bronze leaves, single fragrant flowers and bean-like, fleshy fruits to 25cm in length.

The Philippine Caper Tree, **C. micrantha,** is widely distributed from India, through Malaysia to the Philippines. It is an erect, thorny small tree to 5m in height, and with drooping branches. Its shining leaves are oblong, deeply-veined, and 17cm long. The exquisite flowers appear right along the branches, developing above the leaf-axils. The small petals are only 1cm in length and generally white, though one may be marked in red or yellow. From the centre of the flower emerges a group of fine white stamens, in spectacular display.

Capparis micrantha
Halobagat, Cat's Whisker

Cassia multijuga
Golden Shower Tree

CASSIA

Senna or Shower Tree,
Pudding-pipe Tree
* **Mostly deciduous/fast**
* **All seasons/long blooming/fragrant**
* **Ht: 7-20m/20-60ft**

|T| |H|

Possibly the most attractive of warm-climate tree genera, the Sennas or **Cassias** are certainly the most widespread. There are between four and five hundred species, native to all subtropical areas of both Northern and Southern Hemispheres, and blooming in a wide spectrum of colours.

Not all **Cassias** are trees, of course. There are shrubs, climbers and perennials among them, but the tree species are by far the most numerous and spectacular. They all like an open sunny position and seem to do best in well-drained soil of a warm to tropical climate, though many of the North American and Australian species are reasonably frost hardy.

Cassias are a large sub-division of the pea family, Leguminosae, and in spite of their great variety have a number of points in common. They have pinnate leaves with a variable number of small leaflets appearing alternately down the leaf stalk. The flowers are five-petalled and open, with prominent stamens. They are most commonly yellow, but are also found in red,

CASSIA (continued)

orange, white or pink.

In some species the flowers appear in long, weeping sprays, and in others are rigid spikes at the end of branchlets. Some are perfumed, some not, and they cross-pollinate indiscriminately, producing many lovely hybrids.

Though different **Cassia** species flower in different seasons, almost every one is

Cassia surattensis
Singapore Shower

Cassia brewsteri
Cigar Cassia

Cassia spectabilis
Golden Wonder

Cassia X *hybrida*
Rainbow Shower

Cassia javanica
Apple Blossom Cassia

Cassia fistula
Pudding-pipe Tree

CASSIA (continued)

capable of gorgeous display for weeks or months on end, carpeting the ground all around with colourful blossom. The flowers are followed by long pea-like pods which are up to 60cm long in some species. These are a rich source of tannin and of medicinal senna. From a gardener's point of view, the pods are the only disadvantage, hanging in unsightly masses from the branches, and finally littering the grass below.

Cassias are mostly fast growers, raised easily from seed, and their wide range means that there are suitable species for almost all gardening climates. While we are only able to illustrate a few of the best, these pictures should give some idea of the group's potential.

The name **Cassia** is from the Hebrew *quetsi'oth*.

CASTANOSPERMUM

Moreton Bay Chestnut,
Black Bean
* **Semi-deciduous**/slow
* **Summer**
* **Ht: to 20m/60ft**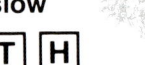

Named Moreton Bay Chestnuts by early British settlers, these handsome Australian trees actually have only one point of similarity to the European Chestnuts — the size and shape of their nuts, which may be roasted and eaten.

Botanists followed the settlers' lead and christened the tree **Castanospermum,** meaning chestnut-seeded. Beyond that, there is no resemblance or relationship at all. The leaves are smooth-edged and compound, growing up to 45cm in length, with five to seven pairs of leaflets. The flowers are typical pea flowers of orange and red, borne in sprays directly from the trunk or branches. These are followed by equally cylindrical pea pods up to 23cm long and about a quarter as wide. Each contains a number of the large, edible seeds.

C. australe is a handsome tree in its own right, with dense, dark foliage for most of the year but becoming partly deciduous as the flowers appear in summer. It is slow-growing, propagated from seeds or ripe cuttings, and is now raised in many warm-temperate parts of the world.

Strictly a tree for frost-free areas, it makes a striking garden specimen or street tree where there is plenty of room. It is very variable in habit, but generally wide and spreading in the open.

The timber is greatly valued and has been used for fine furniture, under the name Black Bean.

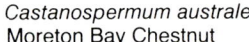

Castanospermum australe
Moreton Bay Chestnut

Catalpa bignonioides
Indian Bean

CATALPA

Indian Bean, Cigar Tree, Catawba
* **Deciduous/medium**
* **Summer/fragrant**
* **Ht: 15-35m/45-100ft**

C T

The showy **Catalpas** or Indian Beans are lush trees of a most tropical appearance, and it is something of a surprise to find that they are all native to northern climates (Asia and North America) and are relatively frost-resistant.

This is the tree for your sunny lawn. And if you like heart-shaped leaves, they don't come any larger than the massive 30cm beauties that clothe this splendid tree most of the year. New growth is purplish; mature leaves may be green or golden according to variety. They have a slightly furry texture, and, unfortunately, in most species a rather unpleasant smell when crushed.

The foxglove-like summer flowers appear in large fragrant clusters or spikes — white, pink or lemon according to species, generally marked in purple or yellow. These are followed by long, dangling pods which give **Catalpas** their popular names of Indian Bean and Cigar Tree.

Catalpas are easily propagated from seed, summer cuttings, layers, or grafting Just be sure to allow plenty of room, for they often grow as wide as they grow tall.

C. speciosa is the largest, reaching 35m — a very wide-crowned tree. Its blossoms are white, spotted purple. **C. bignonioides** has similar flowers, grows to 15m. Both are from North America. The Chinese **C. fargesii** grows only to 20m, has rose-pink flowers, striped yellow.

All **Catalpa** timber is water-resistant and is used where it may be in contact with damp earth, but generally of poor quality.

Ceratopetalum gummiferum
NSW Christmas Bush

CERATOPETALUM

NSW Christmas Bush, Coachwood, Redbush
* **Evergreen**/slow
* **Summer**/long display
* **Ht: 12-30m/38-95ft**

In the coastal bushlands of New South Wales, and in many gardens of Australia, the summer Christmas season is announced by a small slender tree, **Ceratopetalum gummiferum.** As spring fades and the longest day approaches, the tree at first becomes powdered with tiny white flowers that appear in the leaf axils. The calyces (seed sheaths) behind them enlarge until they are almost 1cm in diameter, and then begin to change colour, flushing first a soft pink and then darkening in some local varieties to a brilliant cherry red, sometimes flushed with royal purple.

Although it has no practical use, it is beloved throughout its home state and picked lavishly for Christmas decoration. It is generally known as Redbush or Christmas Bush, and so eyecatching is the floral display, few people ever notice that behind it is a dark, slender tree with distinctive trifoliate (three-lobed) leaves of softest green. In

CERATOPETALUM (continued)

positions with deep rich soil (so rare along this coast) it may reach 12m in height.

There are four other **Ceratopetalum** species, native to the humid forests further north. One of them is of considerable importance — the Coachwood, **C. apetalum,** a splendid timber tree which may reach 30m and more.

Both principal species of **Ceratopetalum** are hardy down to −2°C/28°F. They are also grown in the southern United States, usually from ripened cuttings.

CERBERA

Sea Mango
* **Evergreen/fast**
* **Summer**
* **Ht: 7-15m/20-50ft**

Closely related to the Frangipanis (see **Plumeria**), and resembling them in many particulars, the gawky Sea Mangoes or **Cerberas** are native to islands of the Pacific and Indian Oceans, and southern areas of the Indo-Malaysian mainland. They are salt-resistant and often used in tropical seaside gardens where the white, red-marked flowers make a pleasant summer display. These appear in clusters at the ends of the branches, and are followed by tennis-ball-sized green or red fruits.

It would be an unfortunate man who *did* mistake these for mangoes, for like many other members of the Periwinkle family (Apocynaceae), all parts of the plant are poisonous. In fact it is believed that the botanical name **Cerbera** is an allusion to these poisonous qualities — it appears to be an adaptation of the Cerberus, the monstrous guardian of Hell, in Greek myths.

There are six species of **Cerbera**, of which one, **C. odollan,** may reach 15m. Of the other species, **C. manghas** and **C. venenifera** rarely top 7m and have pink to blue fruits. They are propagated from cuttings or seed.

Flowers of all species can easily be mistaken for Frangipanis, but without the strong perfume.

Cerbera manghas
Sea Mango

Cerbera venenifera

CERCIS

Cercis canadensis
Redbud

Cercis siliquastrum
Judas Tree

Judas Tree, Redbud
* **Deciduous/slow**
* **Spring/fragrant**
* **Ht: 5-13m/15-40ft**

To an Australian, spring in the United States is an introduction to a new botanical world. After the generally dull tones of the Australian bush, the awakening forest of north-eastern America is a revelation with its Elms and Dogwoods and Sassafras; and everywhere, glowing in the pale sunlight, spindly many-branched trees covered in every part with brilliant rose-pink blossom. These are the Redbuds, **Cercis canadensis,** showy members of the pea family, Leguminosae.

There are seven **Cercis** species from Europe, Asia and North America, all with a strong family resemblance. They are deciduous, growing from 5m to around 15m in the wild. The leaves are kidney-shaped, and their small pea-flowers, generally pink, but sometimes white or purple, appear on bare wood (often from the trunks or older branches) in stalkless clusters. They are followed by absolute masses of 10cm flat pods, which persist well into winter.

The name **Cercis** is from the Greek *kerkis*, the original name of the European species **C. siliquastrum.** This is sometimes known as the Judas Tree, from an old legend that it was the tree from which Judas Iscariot hanged himself after betraying Christ. In contrast to its cousins, it is fast growing, may develop a columnar or round-headed shape.

Of the other species, only **C. occidentalis** is much grown, and then in its native territory of the western United States. It is particularly slow growing and of a shrubby habit.

C. chinensis, the Chinese Redbud, becomes a 17m tree in its native habitat, though rarely more than a bush when grown in the north-east United States because of its cold-hardiness. Also Chinese, **C. racemosa** has purplish flowers, but is suitable only for warm temperate areas.

None of the genus has any commercial use. All of them are grown for the beauty of their spring blossom, particularly in cooler climates.

CHIONANTHUS

Fringe Tree,
Old Man's Beard
* **Deciduous**/slow
* **Spring-summer**/
  fragrant
* **Ht: 5m/15ft**

C T

An ideal choice for the cool to temperate garden, the slim and delicate Fringe Trees, **Chionanthus,** will never outwear their welcome, being unlikely to top 5m.

Both species are deciduous, one from China, one from North America. The Chinese species **C. retusa** is the more dainty, with slim 10cm pointed leaves, dense panicles of pure white 2.5cm flowers in summer. It is frost-hardy, loves a good woodsy soil in full sun.

The American **C. virginiana** is sometimes called Old Man's Beard, for its flower panicles droop in a pointed fashion to 20cm.

Chionanthus retusa
Chinese Fringe Tree

CHIRANTHODENDRON

Monkey Hand Tree,
Mexican Hand Flower
* **Deciduous**/fast
* **Spring-summer**
* **Ht: to 8m/25ft** T H

Cultivated in southern California and other subtropical regions is the curious Monkey Hand Tree, **Chiranthodendron pentadactyla,** long attributed with magical qualities by Mexican Indians. Fast growing, with gnarled, woody branches and furry leaves like those of the London Plane Tree, it bears some of the most remarkable flowers in the world. Borne in clusters at the leaf axils, often well-hidden by the foliage, a series of bronze, furry buds appear, very like those of **Brachychiton discolor** (which see). One by one, these develop into cup-sized dull red flowers from the centre of which emerges a blood-red, hand-shaped appendage, complete with sharp, curved claws. These do look like the monkey's hand with which Mexican superstition has identified them. **Chiranthodendron** needs rich soil, plenty of water.

Chiranthodendron pentadactyla
Monkey Hand Tree

FLOWERING TREES

Choricarpia leptopetala
Brush Turpentine

Chorisia insignis
Spiny Chorisia

CHORICARPIA

Brush Turpentine
* **Deciduous/fast**
* **Spring**
* **Ht: 16m/50ft**   [T] [H]

A fine ornamental for warm coastal areas, **Choricarpia leptopetala** has been little known outside Australia, though it would suit many climates. It will grow to 16m and is quite similar to the closely related Turpentine (see **Syncarpia**) in whose genus it was once included.

The leaves are smooth, leathery and wavy-edged, rust coloured when young, but ripening to a soft green with rusty reverse. The spring blossoms, each on a long stem, appear in large arching clusters in mid-spring, great puffballs of creamy stamens similar to Wattle, but much larger.

Choricarpia (the name means separate fruits) flowers when quite young, at which stage it may be mistaken for **Callicoma** (which see). However, the leaves are quite different.

The beautiful Brush Turpentine has proved itself an ideal street tree in warm temperate parts of Australia.

CHORISIA

Floss Silk Tree
* **Deciduous/fast**
* **Autumn**
* **Ht: to 17m/50ft**   [T] [H]

Unless you can get some viable seed from South America and grow **Chorisia** for yourself, you're not likely to have one. Not that the climate is unsuitable — they will grow wherever the winter temperature remains above −7°C/19°F — but they rarely want to set seed away from their natural home, and won't grow from cuttings. Yet I have seen them in Sydney, in California, in Florida and in Samoa among other places, and the sight of a **Chorisia** in full bloom is food for the soul — no two of them with flowers exactly the same.

That is their peculiarity. The 15cm flowers on one giant tree will always differ from those on another, both in colour and in

Chorisia speciosa

Chorisia speciosa
Floss Silk Tree

CHORISIA (continued)

structure. In the case of the best-known species, the Brazilian **C. speciosa,** the flowers will be five-petalled and basically pink and resemble the related **Hibiscus;** but beyond that they may vary from reddish to salmon in colour, their centres white or yellow, marked in deep red or brown, the petals plain or with rippled edges. That adds up to an enormous range of possible variations.

The related **C. insignis** from Peru has basically white flowers, marked with gold, but they may also be all yellow or marked in various colours.

Both these species grow tall, 15m and more, and have tapering trunks up to 2m in diameter at ground level. These are liberally studded with a nightmare arrangement of barbaric thorns and spines and would be impossible to climb. **C. speciosa** tends to grow straight, with a high spreading crown of branches; **C. insignis** branches quite close to the ground.

The leaves of both species consist of five or seven leaflets spread like the fingers of a hand, and often toothed. Superficially they resemble those of a Horse Chestnut (see **Aesculus**) and are deciduous in late summer. The flowers appear on bare branches in autumn.

Cochlospermum vitifolium
Maximiliana

COCHLOSPERMUM

Maximiliana,
Buttercup Tree
* **Deciduous/fast**
* **Winter**
* **Ht: to 10m/30ft**

I know of no larger, brighter yellow flowers than those of Mexico's showy Buttercup Tree. At home wherever the climate is really hot, **Cochlospermum** grows easily from cuttings or seed in warm weather.

It is slender and deciduous, will begin flowering when a mere metre high, although it may ultimately reach 10m after a number of years. A rather sparse and stiff-looking tree, its leaves are larger than a dinner plate. They are five-lobed (rather like those of a grape vine or **Liquidambar**), and appear in spring after the tree's three-month blooming period.

It is in late winter that the **Cochlospermum** achieves its finest moment, as golden-yellow, cup-sized blossoms open a few at a time, rapidly carpeting the ground as they fall. They are five-petalled, with a mass of golden stamens.

C. vitifolium, the best-known species of eighteen recorded, is seen in hot climate gardens of India, the Philippines, Africa, California and Florida. Its cousin **C. religiosum** from India is virtually identical. Australian species **C. gillevraei** has bright red flowers.

COMAROSTAPHYLIS

Summer Holly
* **Evergreen**/fast
* **Late spring**/ fragrant
* **Ht: to 7m/20ft**

Not the most spectacular tree in the world, the Summer Holly **(Comarostaphylis diversifolia)** is widely grown in its native southern California and nearby Mexican states. It is a dry-climate relative of the Irish Strawberry and Madrone (see **Arbutus**), and should be seen more often in gardens of the Mediterranean, South Africa, Australia and other similar climatic areas. It is an erect, slender tree with grey bark and leathery 7.5cm evergreen leaves, dark and shiny above, woolly-white beneath, with the leaf-margins generally rippled and rolled inward. Small, white **Arbutus**-like flowers appear in terminal panicles in late spring. They are mildly fragrant and followed by clusters of bright-red, warty fruits, also like those of the **Arbutus**. These ripen in midsummer, and give the tree the appearance of out-of-season holly. **Comarostaphylis** is a most adaptable small tree, but seems to do best in a sheltered, partly-shaded position with excellent drainage. Do not overwater.

Comarostaphylis diversifolia
Summer Holly

Cordia sebestena
Bird Lime Tree

CORDIA

Bird Lime Tree, Kou
* **Evergreen**/fast
* **All year**
* **Ht: to 10m/30ft** T H

Cordia are showy tropical relatives of the temperate gardener's forget-me-nots and heliotrope, and like them easy to grow and almost trouble-free. There are at least 250 listed species, all of them found between the tropics of both the old and new worlds, in Africa, Asia, Australia and particularly in the Americas.

The commonly seen species is **C. sebestena,** the Geiger or Bird Lime Tree from the Caribbean. This is notable for its

CORDIA (continued)

rough 20cm oval leaves, whose dark colouring makes a perfect foil for the vivid orange-scarlet flowers, which are borne in terminal clusters throughout the year. The Bird Lime Tree grows easily from seed or cuttings in a sub-tropical climate, reaching 10m in just a few years. It is most spectacular, and a yellow-flowered variety is sometimes seen.

Its paler-flowered cousin **C. subcordata** is the sacred Kou tree of Polynesia, found by seashores throughout the Indian and Pacific Oceans. There is a legend that when a downpour of rain threatened to extinguish fire, the beloved Polynesian god Maui told the flames to take refuge in the Kou tree, hence the colour of its flame-orange blossom!

C. subcordata has smooth, paler, wavy-edged leaves, and slightly less gaudy flowers which are followed by green and yellow grape-sized fruits. The figured timber was used in Polynesia for carving sacred figures and household utensils.

Cordias are named for a sixteenth century family of botanists named Cordus.

Cordia subcordata
Kou

CORDYLINE

Cabbage Tree, Palm Lily
* Evergreen/slow
* Late spring/fragrant
* Ht: to 10m/30ft

Like the closely related Chinese Good Luck Plant **(Dracaena fragrans),** this interesting New Zealander can be propagated from 10cm sections of stem laid in sand. Not a true tree, **Cordyline stricta** is a woody palm-like plant, valued for landscaping effect in temperate climates. Slow-growing, it begins life as a fountain of narrow 1m leaves, but gradually develops a trunk, and much later, branches. Professional landscape artists cut it back periodically when young to force multiple trunks, lower branches. In late spring, each head of foliage develops branching clusters of tiny, fragrant 5mm flowers, sometimes with a mauve tint. It will grow in any soil deep enough for its extended roots, is extremely drought resistant. Variety **atropurpurea** has purplish-bronze leaves.

Cordyline australis
Cabbage Tree

CORNUS

Cornel, Dogwood
* **Deciduous**/fast
* **Spring**
* **Ht: 5-12m/15-40ft**

I shall never forget my first train ride to Virginia, speeding on the Powhatan Arrow through the Allegheny Mountains in the clear light of an April morning. All along the valley route, the landscape was touched with spring — dark coal-mining towns alternating with a riot of lime-green foliage, fern and fuzz. And here and there against the drab rocks the brilliance of a million flowering dogwoods, white, pink and almost red.

It was only later, in a friend's garden in Roanoke, that I discovered the inflorescence of the common Flowering Dogwood **(Cornus florida)** is not a flower at all, but a whole composite head of tiny greenish flowers with four spectacularly marked bracts enclosing the group.

When the bracts fall, the flowers develop into a cluster of bright red fruits which persist into autumn, joining the foliage in a fiery farewell to summer.

C. florida is a slim, dark-trunked tree growing from 5 to 12m in height, its crepey, pointed leaves marked with conspicuous parellel veins.

There are around a hundred species of Dogwood found in cool-winter temperate parts of America and Asia, many of them shrubs with brilliantly coloured winter bark, sometimes red, white or yellow.

Other tree species of note include: **C. capitata,** a widely branched Himalayan tree of 15m, and partly evergreen. The bracts are creamy white, the fruit like a rather large raspberry. **C. controversa,** the Giant Dogwood from the Himalayas, grows to 20m. Leaves whitish beneath. Masses of

Cornus florida alba
White Dogwood

Cornus florida
Flowering Dogwood

CORNUS (continued)

pinkish flowers with cream bracts in summer. **C. kousa,** a small Japanese tree of 7m, deciduous, with dense masses of creamy-pink, bracted blossoms in early summer. **C. mas,** the Cornelian Cherry, another small tree from Europe and Asia. Deciduous, with yellow flowers and dark red edible fruits. It has many highly coloured leaf varieties.

The curious brown markings at the bract tips of **C. florida** were at one time given a mystic explanation by early American settlers — who conceived that they were a representation of Christ's nail-wounds at the Crucifixion.

Cornus kousa
Japanese Dogwood

Couroupita guianensis
Cannonball Tree

COUROUPITA

Cannonball Tree
* **Deciduous/fast**
* **Summer/fragrant**
* **Ht: to 17m/30ft**

[H]

Thank goodness Cannonball trees are not to be found in every garden! Dodging the head-size fruit as they come tumbling down in every rainstorm could become a real hazard! They are a sight, though, that every tree-lover wants to see at least once in a lifetime, and all the great warm-climate arboreta make sure we have the chance.

The flower display, too, is a real botanical conversation piece! A 17m tall column decked with slender flower stems all twisted and tangled like Medusa's snake hair! In season, they are decked with Hibiscus-sized blooms of rich apricot pink and gold. These have a curious lopsided mass of stamens and exude a strong fruity fragrance that can be smelt from afar.

The brown, velvety fruits, when they appear in winter, cluster from top to bottom of the tree. They consist of a mass of seeds embedded in sickly pulp, which to Westerners smells distinctly 'off'.

The Cannonball tree is botanically **Couroupita guianensis** — its old name in Guiana, where this curiosity grows wild.

Canonball Trees can be grown easily from seed in a warm climate. Just don't plant one in your garden!

CRATAEGUS

Hawthorn, May
* **Deciduous**/fast
* **Spring**/fragrant
* **Ht: 8-10m/25-30ft**

Gives not the hawthorn bush a sweeter shade
Than doth a rich embroidered canopy?
Good old Shakespeare! As usual, he said it all, signalling his approval of the ubiquitous hedgerow tree of English fields, **Crataegus monogyna,** the common Hawthorn or May.

Planted throughout the British Isles, its thorny branches make an effective barrier to man and beast, but in spring it bursts into clouds of sharp-scented, rose-like blossom.

Frost brings a blaze of autumn colour and a fine crop of red fruits.

Yet the Common Hawthorn is only one of a thousand species of these deciduous members of the rose family.

They all prefer a cooler climate and are frost-hardy. Most have decorative foliage, frequently associated with the most vicious thorns in the botanical kingdom.

The English Hawthorn, **C. oxyacantha,** has many flower varieties, both single and double, red, pink and variegated. Its strain 'Rosea Plena' is double pink, 'Coccinea Plena' and 'Paulii' double red.

All species grow easily from seed, which takes two years to ripen. Grafting is used for fancy strains.

Crataegus oxyacantha
English Hawthorn

DAIS

South African Daphne
* **Deciduous/slow**
* **Spring/fragrant**
* **Ht: to 6.5m/20ft** T H

Though definitely a tree in the hot dry areas of South Africa to which it is native, lovely **Dais cotinifolia** often tends to adopt a shrubby, multiple-trunked habit in the home garden — probably due to the availability of extra water and the absence of leaf-eating animals that prey on its young foliage in the wild. Best follow nature's example and force it into a single trunk when young — though it still may not grow above 4m in height. It is a handsome, slender treelet with reddish bark and blue-green leaves to 7.5cm in length. These are broader towards the tip than at their short stalks, and though South Africans insist it is evergreen, I find it loses its foliage briefly in both Australia and the United States. Apart from some commercial use of the tough bark fibres, **Dais** is grown most for its fragrant, unusual blossom. Tubular pink flowers appear in a dense pompon-shaped cluster in late spring, tend to hang on the tree long after they've faded. A charmer for the small temperate garden.

Dais cotinifolia
South African Daphne

Davidia involucrata
Handkerchief Tree

DAVIDIA

Dove Tree,
Handkerchief Tree
* **Deciduous/fast**
* **Spring**
* **Ht: to 13m/40ft** C T

Just over seventy years ago, the beautiful **Davidia involucrata** caused a botanical sensation when it flowered for the first time in the West in the garden of a French collector named de Vilmorin. This came as the climax of a race between French and English botanists to find and flower a tree reported from western China by the French missionary, Pere David. It had ghostly white flowers fluttering among the foliage like handkerchiefs, or so he reported.

The race and its result are botanical history, but even before the trees were located and taken back to Europe, the botanical name was never in doubt — **Davidia.**

Davidia will grow in any frost-free area short of the subtropics, preferring a deep, rich, acid soil. It may reach 13m but is usually only half that in the average garden. The flower heads are less than 2cm wide, and consist of a number of greenish filaments topped with red or dark-brown stamens. These heads are each surrounded by two unequal bracts, the larger as big as a human hand.

The floral display starts just as the tree opens its spring foliage and lasts for several weeks, after which inedible purplish fruit appear on long stems.

Delonix regia
Royal Poinciana

DELONIX

Poinciana, Flamboyant
* **Deciduous/fast**
* **Summer**
* **Ht: to 10m/30ft**

Believed to have originated on the island of Madagascar, home of so many wonderful plants, **Delonix regia,** the Poinciana or Flamboyant has often been hailed as the showiest flowering tree in the world. But gardeners living further than 30° either north or south of the equator will have to be content to dream about it.

When it does condescend to blossom, it is just like a fireworks display, as the whole tree drops its foliage and lights up literally overnight into a canopy of bright scarlet flowers, each about the size of a rose. These are quite variable in colour, shading from almost crimson to almost orange, in each case with one petal heavily spotted in either white or yellow. There is even a much rarer form, which I photographed in Tahiti, where the entire flower is yellow, one petal marked in cream.

Delonix regia
Yellow form

Delonix regia

The Poinciana (its botanical name **Delonix** is from the Greek **delos,** meaning 'obvious', and it certainly is hard to miss!) is not tall as trees go. Its limit is about 10m but it may ultimately reach three times that in width, a great spreading umbrella that makes wonderful shade in tropical gardens: (see our title page).

The smooth grey trunk often develops large supporting buttresses; the bipinnate leaves are feathery and delicate, like those of a **Jacaranda.**

The flowers are followed by a mass of long, bean-like pods that persist for months.

Diploglottis cunninghamii
Native Tamarind

DIPLOGLOTTIS

Native Tamarind
* **Evergreen/fast**
* **Autumn**
* **Ht: to 17m/50ft** T H

Little known outside Australia, the Native Tamarind, **Diploglottis cunninghamii,** is a handsome evergreen tree from forests of the warm east coast, and could be of great value in warm temperate gardens all over the world. It grows to 17m, a tall, upright tree with a rounded head, and bears enormous 55cm compound leaves, each consisting of up to twelve ruffled leaflets.

The tiny yellow autumn flowers appear in decorative many-branched panicles at the end of branchlets, and are followed by yellow three-celled fruit, the size of a grape. These are full of red juicy, jelly-like pulp, which makes a very acid, but pleasant drink, quite refreshing on hot days. If too sour for your taste, the pulp can be boiled with sugar and water. The native Tamarind also makes delicious jams and chutneys, much like the Asiatic Tamarind (see **Tamarindus**), after which it has been popularly named.

Diploglottis is grown from seed, and its botanical name means 'double tongue', a reference to a minor flower detail apparent only to a botanist.

There are several other species, but none of them seems to be in cultivation.

DOMBEYA

Natal Cherry, Wild Pear, Mexican Rose
* **Deciduous**/fast
* **Autumn-spring**/fragrant
* Ht: 8-15m/25-45ft

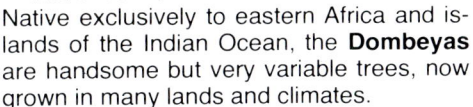

Native exclusively to eastern Africa and islands of the Indian Ocean, the **Dombeyas** are handsome but very variable trees, now grown in many lands and climates.

They include the striking **D. tiliacea** or Natal Cherry, a slim many-trunked tree which may reach 8m. It produces a magnificent display in autumn when the entire tree becomes weighed down with clusters of white fragrant flowers, very similar to the Japanese Cherry Blossom.

D. spectabilis, the Wild Pear, is deciduous, with glossy pear-like foliage, rusty on the underside. The white or pale pink blossom forms dense panicles in spring, often before the leaves.

In warmer climates you'll see the curious Mexican Rose, **D. wallichii,** a small tree which may reach 10m. The crowded pink to scarlet flowers appear in ball-shaped clusters on long, hairy, hanging stems.

Dombeya spectabilis
Wild Pear

Dombeya wallichii
Mexican Rose

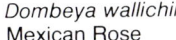

Dombeya tiliacea
Natal Cherry

Drimys winteri
Winter's Bark

DRIMYS

Winter's Bark
* **Evergreen/medium**
* **Spring/fragrant**
* **Ht: to 15m/45ft** C T

Members of this handsome, variable genus of some 40 species within the Magnolia family are found naturally in Central and South America, in Australasia and Indonesia — but only one tree species, the delightful **Drimys winteri** from Chile and Argentina is much cultivated in the garden. Mildly frost-tender, it prefers a moist coastal climate, but will grow well in a sheltered position in warmer areas given plenty of water. Growing to 15m in the wild, it will rarely pass half that in cultivation: a slender, red-trunked tree that is fragrant in all its parts. Like many Magnolias it often tends to a multi-trunked habit, but can easily be pruned and trained to a single trunk with gracefully drooping branches. Both shining, leathery leaves (to 25cm in length) and young red bark are pleasantly aromatic, while the creamy-white 3cm blossoms are considered to share the fragrance of Jasmine. Each flower has between 6 and 12 petals, and they are borne in long-stalked clusters of 7 or 8 blooms.

ELAEAGNUS

Wild Olive, Silverberry
* **Deciduous/slow**
* **Late spring/fragrant**
* **Ht: 6m/18ft**

Known commonly for many shrubby species, the genus **Elaeagnus** also includes several flowering trees, notably **E. angustifolia,** the Oleaster, and **E. umbellata,** the Chinese Silverberry or Wild Olive. It is a handsome, spreading tree with a silver-scaled effect both on young wood and on leaf reverses. In spring, clusters of creamy, tubular flowers spread fragrance all around. These are followed by 5mm fruits that also have a silver-scaly appearance until they ripen to pink. It is found naturally from the Himalayas to Japan.

Eleagnus umbellata
Wild Olive

ELAEOCARPUS

Blueberry Ash, Hinau, Silver Quandong
* **Evergreen/fast**
* **Spring/fragrant**
* **Ht: 8-30m/25-60ft**

Elaeocarpus is a small genus of evergreen flowering trees confined to the Indo-Malaysian area, Australia and New Zealand. Mostly slender, graceful and rather slow-growing at the outset, they bear laurel-like leaves, sometimes toothed.

The fragrant flowers are borne in small sprays like lily-of-the-valley. They are usually white or pink and most delicately fringed. This spring display is followed by a heavy crop of brilliant blue fruits which persist into winter — the botanical name is from the Greek words for 'olive' and 'fruit'.

Species in cultivation include: **E. denticulatus,** New Zealand's Hinau, with pale yellow flowers; **E. grandis,** the Silver Quandong from eastern Australia, with creamy flowers; **E. kirtonii,** the Pigeonberry Ash with white flowers; **E. reticulatus,** the Blueberry Ash, pink or white blossom; and the Malaysian **E. serratus** or Blue Olive Berry with white flowers.

All prefer moist, shaded conditions.

Elaeocarpus reticulatus
Blueberry Ash

Eriobotrya deflexa
Loquat

Erythrina caffra
Kaffirboom

ERIOBOTRYA

Loquat, Japanese Medlar
* **Evergreen/fast**
* **Autumn/fragrant**
* **Ht: 8m/25ft**   T H

Raised in temperate to tropical climates both as an ornamental and for its succulent winter fruits, the Loquat or Japanese Medlar is out of favour in many areas because fruitfly larvae may use it to over-winter. But provided attention is paid to spraying (particularly when the fruit is beginning to form) there is no reason why it should not be grown.

Only a small tree, rarely above 8m in height, it is closely related to apples, pears, quinces and other fruiting trees of the rose family. The rather brittle dark foliage is evergreen, each slightly toothed leaf 25cm long, deeply veined and woolly beneath. The small five-petalled flowers are whitish, fragrant, and appear on rusty, woolly stems at branch tips in the autumn. The fruits ripen at various times in winter according to variety and location. They are the size of a ping-pong ball, slightly oval and pale apricot in colour. Just rub off the slightly downy coating and eat them straight from the tree. They are very succulent, with a sweetly acid flavour, each containing several large slippery seeds.

The Loquat is known botanically as **Eriobotrya** from the Greek words **erion** meaning 'wool' and **botrys** meaning 'a cluster' — an apt description of its flower display. It is native to China and southern Japan, and is popular in southern Europe, southern and western USA, Australia, Africa and many other places.

ERYTHRINA

Coral Tree, Tiger Claw, Kaffirboom
* **Deciduous/fast**
* **Winter-spring**
* **Ht: 5-20m/15-60ft**   T H

There are some who say that the showy **Erythrinas** make an appropriate floral symbol for Los Angeles, the mighty city of

Erythrina variegata
Coral Bean

Erythrina crista-galli
Cockscomb Coral

ERYTHRINA (continued)

the Angels. All show and magnificence on top, they stand on a shaky foundation.

They really are pretty vulnerable. Their wood is poor, weak stuff. The trees are likely to drop a branch without notice, or fall over in a high wind.

At any rate, Los Angeles has adopted them, and they are now planted there in a great variety, though none of them is found naturally in that part of the world.

Native to many other warm temperate and tropical areas in Africa, Central America, Australia, southern Asia, the East Indies and Hawaii, they are mostly gnarled and rugged-looking trees with vicious thorns. Their wood is very light and useless for woodworking. They enjoy best a climate on the warm, dry side, but seem indifferent to winter cold short of frost. The flowers are mostly in brilliant scarlet, in some species shading to crimson and orange, many flowering in mid-winter when the trees are bare of foliage.

Australia's ubiquitous Indian Coral Bean, **E. variegata,** can be struck from large branches as an 'instant tree', but is just as likely to fall over without protection from

Erythrina variegata
Indian Coral Bean

Erythrina speciosa
Corallodendron

Erythrina acanthacarpa
Tambookie Thorn

Erythrina falcata
Coral Tree

ERYTHRINA (continued)

windy weather. Its large heart-shaped leaves give wonderful summer shade. It has a variegated form, **parcellii,** which is known as the Variegated Tiger Claw.

The picturesque **E. crista-galli** or Cockscomb Coral will in time develop a wonderfully gnarled trunk, but (at least in its younger days) will need annual pruning back to the main branches. It bears spikes of scarlet to crimson pea-blossoms at branch ends, in spring.

E. caffra, the Kaffirboom from South Africa, makes a tall, handsome foliage tree and is deservedly popular. Its flowers are vermilion, borne in rounded clusters.

Australia's Batswing Coral, **E. vespertilio,** bears trifoliate leaves that remind one of a bat when seen at an angle. The salmon-pink pea flowers are in erect spikes.

E. falcata produces scarlet bloom in long, hanging clusters.

Eucalyptus caesia
Gungunnu

Eucalyptus racemosa
Narrow-leaf Ironbark

EUCALYPTUS

Eucalypt, Gum Tree [T]
* **Evergreen/fast**
* **All year** [H]
* **Ht: 8-50m/25-250ft**

In Australia, the ubiquitous Gum Tree is king. To all points of the compass, and in the central desert, the great bulk of the continent's natural tree-life consists of one or another of the 600 and more recorded species of **Eucalyptus**. Often very localized by species, the Gums as a group are highly adaptable, and in fact astonishingly adapted to the rigours of life in many diverse climates.

Some flourish in swamps, others eke out a sparse existence in barren deserts where the rainfall in one year may be nil. There are low, scrubby, many-trunked types in the sandplains; tall, needle-straight giants in the forests of Western Australia, Victoria and Tasmania.

The great River Red Gums send out a labyrinth of roots near water, helping combat erosion; the gnarled and hardy Snow Gums twist and sprawl on the lee side of mountains high above the snowline.

The Eucalypts have become Australia's most influential export. You'll find them all over California, in Israel, north, east and South Africa, all about the Mediterranean, and in islands as far apart as Hong Kong and Hawaii.

Eucalypts yield several valuable oils, and because of the enormous quantities of flowers they bear, are an important source of honey.

Eucalypt leaves vary widely according to species, both in length and in width, ranging all the way from spear-shaped to heart-shaped, with often a recognizably different leaf-shape in juvenile foliage, which makes them very tricky to identify.

Their flower display is often quite stunning, though somewhat irregular, and the range of colour goes all the way from crimson through scarlet to palest pink, from white through yellow to orange — though cream is probably the most common. The blooms are completely without petals, and consist of a great mass of stamens. Hybrids of the Western Australian **E. ficifolia** have the showiest and most spectacular flowers of all.

Eucalyptus ficifolia
Red-flowering Gum

Eucalyptus erythrocorys
Illyarie

Eucalyptus microcorys
Tallow-wood

Eucalyptus torquata
Coral Gum

EUCALYPTUS (continued)

Typically, blossoms are small, and appear in large clusters at branch tips or leaf axils, though in at least two Western Australian species, the blooms are borne singly and are as large as a **Camellia.**

The blooms of all Eucalypts have at least one feature found on no other tree, and that is the peculiar cup-shaped lid or operculum which covers each bud. This pops off and drops as the dense mass of stamens expands for the seasonal display. The pictures shown can give only a suggestion of the glorious flower colour varieties and of the vast range of this group of plants.

Eucalypts are usually grown from seed, and accordingly their flower colours and leaf-shapes are notoriously unstable. They are fast growers in garden conditions, and curiously grow quicker from small seedlings than from larger nursery-bought plants.

In common with much other Australian flora they resent cultivation in their vicinity, are best planted by themselves. They have one peculiarity of growth which is virtually unique in the tree world. This is the lignotuber, a vast bulb-like growth which develops at or just below ground level in many species. It serves as a storage chamber for many plant nutrients and allows the tree to survive a dry season or even regenerate completely after devastating fires have destroyed all above-ground growth.

Eucalyptus ficifolia
in California

Eucalyptus leucoxylon rosea
Pink-flowered Whitewood

Eucalyptus rhodantha
Rose Gum

Fagraea berteriana
Pua keni-keni

FAGRAEA

Pua Keni-keni,
Ten Cent Flower
  * **Evergreen/fast**
  * **Warm weather/fragrant**
  * **Ht: to 12m/40ft**

Found naturally right across the Pacific from Queensland to Hawaii, **Fagraea berteriana** is relatively uncommon in cultivation, though universally admired for the fragrance of its flowers which are used by islanders both to perfume oil and to weave greatly-prized leis for special occasions. The tree on which these blooms appear is most variable, ranging from a single-trunked 12m giant in some areas, to a shrubby, many-trunked bush in others, where the soil is not so rich. The Hawaiians sanctified the tree to the God Tane, and his temple images were carved from its hard, white wood.

Short-stemmed leaves are widest at the outer end and up to 15cm long; the fragrant, long-tubed blossoms (cream fading to orange) resemble those of Australia's **Hymenosporum** (which see), and appear at any time during the warm weather. They are followed by smooth oval 2.5cm fruits, each containing many seeds. The fruit ripens from green to red if it gets the chance, but birds find them tasty.

FLINDERSIA

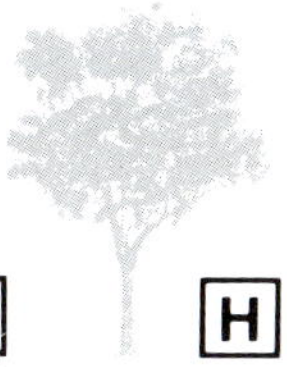

The Australian Ash
* **Evergreen**/fast
* **Late spring**/fragrant
* **Ht: 13-50m**/40-150ft

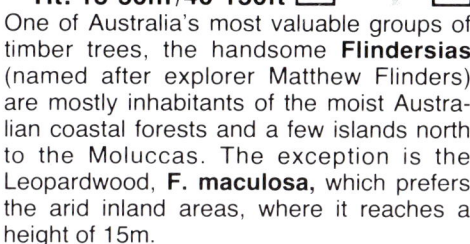

One of Australia's most valuable groups of timber trees, the handsome **Flindersias** (named after explorer Matthew Flinders) are mostly inhabitants of the moist Australian coastal forests and a few islands north to the Moluccas. The exception is the Leopardwood, **F. maculosa,** which prefers the arid inland areas, where it reaches a height of 15m.

The coastal **Flindersias** are much larger trees. Old specimens have been recorded towering to 50m, particularly in Queensland rain forests.

Most of them make splendid specimen or street trees in frost-free areas, and have foliage closely resembling that of the European and American Ash trees (see **Fraxinus**). That is to say, the leaves are compound, consisting of a number of coarse leaflets. Beyond that they vary greatly, bearing masses of small white flowers in late spring. These appear in branching terminal clusters, deliciously fragrant with honey.

Commonly seen species include: **F. australis,** the Crow's Ash; **F. pubescens,** the Silver Ash; and **F. schottiana,** the Bumpy Ash. All species are propagated from seed.

Flindersia pubescens
Silver Ash

FREMONTODENDRON

Tree Poppy
* Evergreen/slow
* All year
* Ht: to 7m/20ft C T

Localized in a small area of southern California, Arizona and north-west Mexico, the two showy **Fremontodendrons** make ideal specimens for dryish sheltered gardens with well-drained sandy soil. The species are **F. californicum** and **F. mexicanum**; both reach about 7m and need help from the pruning shears to grow up as a tree rather than a floppy shrub.

Evergreen except in particularly dry years, they produce woolly greyish leaves, generally three-lobed on the Californian form and five-lobed on the Mexican. The Hibiscus-like flowers appear on short spurs along the branches, varying from yellow to orange in colour. Those of the Mexican species are brighter and larger.

Both **Fremontodendrons** (named for Captain Charles Fremont, explorer of the Golden West) are sometimes known as California Tree Poppy, and are propagated from seed and softwood cuttings. They cannot abide a humid climate, but in the right position can be expected to bloom several times a year. Even in England's cool-temperate climate, they will produce quite a spectacular summer show on a southward facing garden wall.

Fremontodendron mexicanum
Tree Poppy

Fuchsia arborescens
Tree Fuchsia

FUCHSIA

Tree Fuchsia
* Evergreen/fast
* Spring/fragrant
* Ht: to 8m/25ft

Native exclusively to the Pacific area, there are over 100 natural species of **Fuchsia**, found right up the western coast of South and Central America, in New Zealand and (surprisingly) in Tahiti. Far and away the majority are shrubby plants, favoured in cool, moist climates and in shaded positions elsewhere. But the genus also contains a handful of trees, and very beautiful they are. Notable among these are **F. boliviana** with dark red flowers and growing to 7m; New Zealand's **F. excorticata** with green and purple blossoms; and the handsome Mexican **F. arborescens,** the Tree Fuchsia of our illustration. This handsome spreading tree (sometimes listed as **F. paniculata**) may grow to 8m in a suitable position, sheltered from frost under taller trees, particularly conifers. It bears shining pointed-elliptic leaves to 20cm in length, and blooms winter and spring, producing masses of starry, long-tubed blooms in terminal panicles to 25cm in diameter. These are a dark wine red, opening to reveal a delicate shade of lavender pink.

88 • FLOWERING TREES

Geijera parviflora
Wilga

Gliricidia sepium
Madre de Cacao

GEIJERA

Wilga [C] [T] [H]
* **Evergreen/fast**
* **All year/fragrant**
* **Ht: 8-20m/25-60ft**

For habitually dry areas of low rainfall, there is a tree with all the grace and charm of the water-loving willows. This is the Wilga, **Geijera parviflora,** a native of Australia's dry inland areas. Californian gardeners have discovered it, as you might expect, and it also seems to be grown in the Mediterranean lands.

Geijera belongs to the same family as the Citrus, though you'd never guess it from the long, grey 15cm leaves and weeping branches. There is a hint of the relationship in the fragrant starry-white flowers, which are borne in open sprays throughout the year. The Wilga's principal value in cultivation is as a shapely ornamental, rarely touching 8m.

GLIRICIDIA

Madre de Cacao
* **Deciduous/fast**
* **Spring**
* **Ht: 8m/25ft**   [H]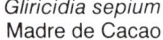

Not the source of cocoa in itself, the picturesque Madre de Cacao (Mother of Cocoa) is regarded in Central America as indispensable for the cultivation of the Cocoa plant. **Gliricidia sepium** is particularly rich in nitrogen. Its falling leaves are turned in around the Cocoa plants as green manure, and its roots are covered in nitrogenous nodules which enrich the soil beneath.

Madre de Cacao grows to 8m, with a short, gnarled trunk and compact, fern-like leaves that drop overnight at the first touch of cold. In early spring the entire tree is decked with charming, perfect pea flowers, mauve-pink with a yellow eye. These appear in small clusters directly from the branches, trunk and twigs.

The tree's botanical name means 'rat poison', for which its seeds are used in Central America and the Philippines.

Gordonia axillaris
Gordonia

GORDONIA

(No common name)
* **Evergreen/slow** [T]
* **Late summer/fragrant**
* **Ht: to 10m/30ft**

Showy **Gordonias** are found in both Asia and North America, and can easily be mistaken for Camellias. Pictured **G. axillaris** makes a handsome tree with shining, broad-ended leaves, and crepe-textured white blooms in the leaf-axils in late summer. These are almost stalkless and drop in a single piece. **Gordonia** is found naturally from Taiwan to Vietnam, and makes a fine garden specimen in deep, rich soil. It remains colourful all winter, when many of its evergreen leaves turn scarlet and gold.

Gordonia axillaris

Grevillea robusta
Silky Oak

GREVILLEA

Silky Oak
* **Deciduous/fast**
* **Summer**
* **Ht: to 50m/150ft** T H

If the Australian flora were known internationally for only a single tree, it would be the glorious Silky Oak, **Grevillea robusta,** which has been an outstanding success both as a street tree and as a garden specimen. You'll find it all over the Mediterranean area, in Africa, the southern United States and in virtually every tropical or subtropical corner of the world. It has been mass-planted as a timber tree in Hawaii, and is raised by millions as one of the world's most desirable indoor plants (though rarely in its native Australia).

A tall grower in nature, where trees of up to 50m have been recorded, the Silky Oak appears spontaneously in the most unlikely places, for its winged seeds can glide for long distances. It has an upright habit with slightly upward-pointing branches decked with silver-backed ferny leaves to 30cm long.

Evergreen in moist climates, it turns deciduous in drier areas, bursting into a razzle-dazzle of vivid orange, comb-like inflorescences in summer. It is so easy to grow from seed you wouldn't think of propagating it any other way.

HAKEA

Pincushion Tree, Sea Urchin
* **Evergreen/slow**
* **Winter/spring**
* **Ht: to 7m/20ft** C T

More cold-hardy than many Australian natives, **Hakea laurina** is happy down to −7°C/20°F. A height of 7m is about the most you can expect, and then only in dry gravelly soils.

Hakea is tremendously popular in the south of France and in California, and occasionally seen pruned to shrubby size as a street tree. But in nature, it is a loose, gangling plant, the branches often weeping and densely covered with leathery blue-green leaves.

The small red flowers are packed in dense 5cm globular heads. Each flower unrolls a single creamy-yellow filament, in a manner typical of the Protea family, until the whole inflorescence resembles a brightly coloured pincushion or sea urchin, both being among its popular names.

Hakea laurina
Pincushion Tree

Hibiscus tiliaceus
Hau

HIBISCUS

Hau, Tree Hibiscus
* **Evergreen/fast** T
* **Warm weather** H
* **Ht: 7m/20ft**

In coastal areas of the world's tropic zone you'll see tangled masses of the Tree Hibiscus, **H. tiliaceus**. But take it into the garden, where the soil is deeper and less saline, and you have a charming warm-climate tree, often with a gnarled, picturesque trunk, and reaching a height of 7m.

The individual leaves are perfectly heart-shaped; during the warm months, flowers appear profusely at the end of every twig, each bud opening spirally to a perfect yellow Hibiscus, usually with a maroon eye. These gradually change to a burnt orange shade, and in the evening become dull red before they drop.

The Hau is winter-hardy down to −4°C/25°F, but only looks its best in a warm, humid climate.

Hymenosporum flavum
Sweet Shade

HYMENOSPORUM

Native Frangipani,
Sweet Shade
* **Evergreen/fast**
* **Spring/fragrant**
* **Ht: to 27m/80ft**

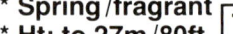

Sweet shade indeed! If fragrance is your fancy, and you live in a climate as warm as coastal Australia, plant a graceful **Hymenosporum flavum** and watch it grow up and up to a height of perhaps 15m, though it can reach 27m in the wild. The foliage is neat, glossy and evergreen, massed alternatively to one side or the other of the tree and at various heights, giving it a marvellous asymmetrical appearance. And in the spring, masses of creamy Frangipani-type flowers tumble out on long stems in a profusion that almost hides the foliage. Delicately marbled with red and green, these ripen to a rich butterscotch shade and spill delicious perfume.

When mature, **Hymenosporum** is reasonably frost-resistant and is found in mountainous districts up to 1000m and more. It apparently tastes as good as it smells, for I once made the mistake of planting one too close to a garden wall, where hungry possums regularly made short work of every flower and leaf.

IPOMOEA

Morning Glory Tree
* **Deciduous/fast**
* **Spring-summer**
* **Ht: to 7m/20ft**

The world of trees is full of the most unlikely contradictions. When first I saw the handsome tree illustrated here I had to revise all my beliefs about Morning Glories being only vines or small groundcovers, for here was one right before my eyes which grows to 7m, has a woody trunk and branches, and yet flowers like you would never believe!

It comes from Mexico and Guatemala, where they call it Palo Blanco, and is known botanically as **Ipomoea arborescens,** a name as unlikely as the plant itself.

The Morning Glory Tree has velvety heart-shaped leaves that are deciduous, and dense clusters of open white trumpet flowers centred in red. Like others of the genus, these open at dawn and fade or drop later in the day. It seems to prefer a cool, not too humid atmosphere.

Ipomoea arborescens
Morning Glory Tree

Itea ilicifolia
Sweetspire

ITEA

Sweetspire
* **Evergreen/fast**
* **Summer/fragrant**
* **Ht: 5m/16ft**

Iteas are a small genus of slim, decorative trees for moist, temperate climates. The species commonly cultivated is the Hollyleaf Sweetspire, **I. ilicifolia,** from western China, which is most at home in deep rich soil of humid coastal gardens.

As both its popular and botanical names suggest, the foliage resembles that of the European Holly. The delicate greenish-white summer flowers are lightly fragrant, and crowded in hanging racemes up to 40cm in length.

I. ilicifolia rarely passes 5m in height except in the most sheltered conditions, and is easily propagated from cuttings of ripe wood taken in summer.

The botanical name **Itea** is the old Greek word for willow, which has a similar habit.

JACARANDA

Blue Haze Tree, Fern Tree
* **Deciduous/fast**
* **Late spring**
* **Ht: to 17m/50ft** T H

The **Jacaranda** is found naturally in the high and dry deserts of Brazil, and many temperate gardeners have noticed that its late spring display is measurably better in a dry year, or in a neglected part of the garden. Give it too much water and the lacy leaves (like pale-green ostrich plumes) appear first, somewhat spoiling the startling effect of mauve trumpet flowers on bare grey branches.

Jacarandas seed readily, grow fast and transplant easily. One in my own garden, a scant ten years from seed, is 8m high and about the same in spread.

Jacarandas are deciduous, though they do not drop their leaves until late winter, often turning a rich yellow first in cooler areas. There are white, pink and red flowered species, but these are not half so lovely as the beautiful mauve-blue **J. mimosaefolia.**

Jacaranda mimosaefolia

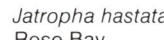
Jatropha hastata
Rose Bay

JATROPHA

Rose Bay, Peregrina
* **Evergreen/fast**
* **Warm weather/fragrant**
* **Ht: to 5m/15ft**

T H

Mostly represented in warm temperate gardens by small shrubs with unbelievably complex leaves, the genus **Jatropha** also includes several highly decorative small trees.

First among these, and now almost universal in its distribution, is the charming Rose Bay or Peregrina, **J. hastata,** from Cuba. Slight in habit, rarely passing 5m in height, the Rose Bay has lightly weeping branches clothed in handsome velvety leaves shaped like a spear blade. The vivid cerise flowers are borne in profuse racemes at the ends of branchlets.

◂ *Jacaranda mimosaefolia*
Blue Haze Tree

96 • FLOWERING TREES

Kigelia pinnata
Sausage Tree

Kleinhovia hospita
Guest Tree

KIGELIA

Sausage Tree
* **Evergreen**/fast
* **Night-blooming**/summer
* **Ht: to 17m/50ft**

Grown only in gardens with a subtropical climate, the curious **Kigelia pinnata** is a heavy-trunked tree of about 16m. It bears compound leaves consisting of between seven and eleven hand-sized leaflets. From the uppermost branches, long hanging stems descend to produce chains of large, night-blooming flowers of velvety red-brown. These have an unpleasant smell and are fertilized by some night-flying insect, after which they drop messily.

What follows is one of the wonders of the botanical world — long, inedible gourd-like fruits up to 1m in length and as thick as your arm. These hang on cord-like stems, contain nothing but hard pulp and seeds.

They are grown from seed or from cuttings of half-ripened wood, and you'll find them in all the warm-climate gardens.

Kigelia is known as the Sausage Tree, for fairly obvious reasons.

KLEINHOVIA

Guest Tree
* **Evergreen**/fast
* **Summer-autumn**
* **Ht: to 20m/60ft**

The tall-growing **Kleinhovia** is a true butterfly of the arboreal world, for its sole function in life seems merely to be admired.

It is native to the whole northern area of the Indian Ocean — Africa, India and Indonesia. It has a rather short, crooked trunk, but skyward-pointing branches which may reach a height of 20m. These spread into a wide crown, decked with long-stalked, rather heart-shaped leaves. The tree produces loose masses of showy pink blossom at its branch tips throughout the summer and autumn.

Kleinhovia hospita is grown from cuttings of young shoots struck in sand.

KOELREUTERIA

Pride of China, [C] [T]
Golden Rain
  * **Deciduous/fast** [H]
  * **Summer bloom/autumn pods**
  * **Ht: to 20m/60ft**

Useful specimen trees for all types of soil and all sorts of climates, the decorative Golden Rain Trees are natives of China and Korea, with one species apparently found in Fiji as well.

They are propagated from seeds or root cuttings, grow rapidly to a height of 15m, less in cooler areas. Full sun and shelter from prevailing wind are main requirements: they are no good near the coast, being damaged by salt breeze.

The branches are decked with 45cm compound leaves, pinnate with toothed leaflets in the species **Koelreuteria paniculata,** fully bipinnate in the species **K. bipinnata** and **K. elegans.**

In summer all three bear branched heads of tiny yellow flowers that scatter as they fall. These are superseded by papery, bladder-like seed pods that persist for months.

Koelreuteria paniculata
Golden Rain Tree

Kopsia fruticosa

KOPSIA

(No popular name)
  * **Evergreen/fast**
  * **Spring/fragrant** [H]
  * **Ht: to 7m/20ft**

Slender, evergreen trees related to Frangipani, several species of **Kopsia** are seen away from their native South East Asia.

K. flavida from Java, a 13m tree with paired, oval leaves and bearing masses of fragrant white flowers. These are followed by black, plum-shaped fruits.

K. fruticosa from Malaysia — a sparsely branched tree of more slender habit, rarely reaching 7m. This has large Plumeria-style leaves that occasionally turn red before they drop, and pale pink, 5-petalled flowers with a red eye, borne in terminal clusters. They look very much like the related annual, **Vinca rosea.**

Laburnum X *vossii*
Golden Chain Tree

LABURNUM

Golden Chain Tree
* **Deciduous/fast**
* **Spring/fragrant**
* **Ht: 10m/25-30ft**

The spring glory of cool-climate gardens where they contrast to perfection with pink and white blossom of peach and apple, the graceful **Laburnums** or Golden Chain Trees are native to central Europe and parts of Asia Minor.

They are deciduous trees of slim, graceful habit with small compound leaves, covered with silky hair on the reverse side. Chains of golden pea flowers (very variable in their brightness) are followed by simple brown pea-type pods.

All species grow well in any type of soil, provided the winters are cold and the atmosphere moist. They self-sow from seed, but named varieties are normally budded, just like roses.

LAGERSTROEMIA

Crepe Myrtle
* **Deciduous**/fast C T
* **Summer**
* **Ht: 7-25m /20-80ft** H

Native to South East Asia and islands of the western Pacific, the showy Crepe Myrtles, **Lagerstroemia,** are some of the most ornamental flowering trees in the world, yet they are so often represented only by hard-pruned, shrub-sized specimens.

Two species only are commonly grown, with a number of colour varieties among them. They are:

L. indica, the Chinese Crepe Myrtle, a slim tree to 7m with four-sided small branches and smooth oval leaves not more than 5cm long. These put up a good autumn colour display in cool districts. The flowers develop at branch tips only, each flower about the size of a peach blossom. On every flower there are six round, wrinkled petals on narrow bases, a mass of gold stamens and a glossy green calyx. There are named flower varieties in red, purple, pink, mauve and white.

Lagerstroemia speciosa
Queen Crepe Myrtle

LAGERSTROEMIA (continued)

L. speciosa, the Queen Crepe Myrtle or Pride of India, is found naturally in a wide belt from India through southern China and Papua New Guinea to Australia. It is a strong-growing tree to 25m with leathery leaves up to 30cm long. The flowers are borne on long-stemmed spikes, each about the size of a Camellia; generally a pleasing rosy-mauve, but sometimes white. The calyx is greyish-pink and downy, and the flowers are followed by woody seed capsules that somtimes persist for months.

Both species can be grown from seed, but more reliably from cuttings. A pruning in winter and another after flowering will give you two flower displays a year. They bloom only on new season's wood.

Lagerstroemia indica
Crepe Myrtle

Lagunaria patersonii
Norfolk Island Hibiscus

LAGUNARIA

Norfolk Island Hibiscus, Pyramid Tree
* **Evergreen/fast**   [T]
* **Warm weather**
* **Ht: to 16m/50ft**   [H]

First discovered on the lonely Pacific penal colony of Norfolk Island in 1792, **Lagunaria patersonii** has a seaside ancestry stretching back thousands of years, and is one of the few trees that can really cope with the salt-laden air of coastal gardens.

Propagated easily from seed, it grows quickly in a warm climate to a maximum height of 16m. The leaves are simple 10cm ovals, almost white on their reverses. Throughout the warm weather, the trees are decked with pretty rose-pink flowers, exactly like small Hibiscus, to which the tree is closely related.

Lagunaria was subsequently rediscovered on remote Lord Howe Island, and on parts of the Queensland coast.

In spite of its predilection for growing in sandy soil, it is not drought-resistant. The flowers vary widely from a deep rose to almost white, sometimes with a tendency towards mauve.

LEPTOSPERMUM

Tea Tree, Manuka
* **Evergreen**/fast
* **Spring**/fragrant
* **Ht: 8-10m/20-30ft**

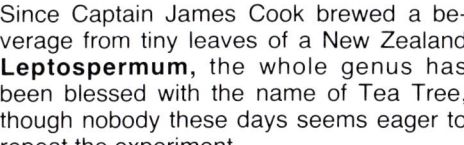

Since Captain James Cook brewed a beverage from tiny leaves of a New Zealand **Leptospermum,** the whole genus has been blessed with the name of Tea Tree, though nobody these days seems eager to repeat the experiment.

New Zealand species **L. scoparium** is the parent of the hybrid, shrubby types seen in so many gardens, with their flower colours varying from white through pinks to deep red; single or double.

But the really useful and decorative tree species is Australian **L. laevigatum,** the Coastal Tea Tree, found in sandy coastal areas of Tasmania, Victoria, New South Wales and well up into Queensland. It is salt and wind-resistant and of tremendous value both as a windbreak in coastal gardens and for stabilizing the movement of drifting sands.

The Coastal Tea Tree grows to 10m and more in a sheltered position, but is most often seen in a variety of contorted shapes, sometimes quite horizontal from its exposure to gales. The bark is stringy, grey and picturesque, the foliage fine and often quite dense. Its oblong, pointed leaves are only about 2.5cm long. The flowers are stalkless, and borne singly in the leaf-axils, making quite a display at many times of the year. Each consists of five rounded white petals surrounding a pale-green ovary which develops into a brown woody seed capsule after fertilization. The capsules often persist on the tree for years.

The Lemon-scented Tea Tree, **L. petersonii,** is also Australian. Its leaves are twice as long, the flowers smaller, but borne in great profusion. A lemon-scented oil is extracted from the foliage.

The botanical name **Leptospermum** is from the Greek **leptos** meaning 'slender', and **sperma** meaning 'seed', in reference to the fine seeds contained in each capsule. Tea Trees grow readily from seed or more commonly from cuttings of half-ripened wood.

Leptospermum laevigatum
Tea Tree

Leptospermum petersonii
Lemon-scented Tea Tree

Ligustrum lucidum
Chinese Privet

Ligustrum ovalifolium
California Privet

LIGUSTRUM

Privet

* **Evergreen/fast**
* **Early summer/fragrant**
* **Ht: 5-10m/15-30ft**

I do not greatly care for Privets myself, having once spent a year hauling them out of a neglected garden. The roots were like a strangling boa constrictor with a grip on everything in sight. And for years afterwards my every gardening effort was thwarted by a crop of tiny new trees from long-discarded berries.

I sometimes wonder why so many garden books waste space on how to propagate them — in my experience propagation is the least of its problems. How do you tell them to stop?

Yet in spite of all this I must admit that the Chinese Privet, **Ligustrum lucidum,** is a handsome tree. Smooth trunked and evergreen, with glossy, pointed leaves up to 15cm long, it is especially beautiful in early summer when the entire tree is frosted with panicles of tiny cream four-petalled flowers like white lilac. It is when these fall and the berries ripen that trouble starts; though again, these fruits are a wonderful glossy purple-black.

If you do want to grow this tree, the ideal place is a fairly neglected part of the garden away from cultivated areas. Just watch those berries, sweep them up before they take hold. Check with your local agricultural authorities too — some areas of Australia and other countries have declared this Chinese invader a noxious pest. Its rampant reproductive habits tend to upset the local ecology.

The California Privet, **L. ovalifolium,** is half the size, in both growth and leaf-shape. It rarely passes 5m in height, is most often seen clipped to a dense hedge or windbreak. Its display of tiny white flowers appears in late spring or early summer, borne in dense, fragrant spikes. Pure heaven to look at — pure hell to the sufferer from hay fever or asthma.

Ligustrum is its ancient Latin name. Several smaller-growing, coloured-leaf varieties are easier to manage.

Liriodendron tulipifera
Tulip Tree

LIRIODENDRON

Tulip Tree, Tulip Poplar
* **Deciduous/fast**
* **Late spring/fragrant**
* **Ht: 25m/80ft**

Closely related to Magnolias, the Tulip Tree, **Liriodendron,** is native to the eastern seaboard of the United States except for northern New England and southern Florida. A fast grower, slow to flower, it may reach 7m in as many years, and ultimately the straight trunk may top 25m.

The deciduous leaves are unique. Long-stemmed and four-lobed, with the appearance of having been lopped off at the apex, they unfurl quite late in spring, well after the Maples, and turn to a blaze of molten gold in autumn.

The name Tulip Tree is in reference to the handsome flowers, which are indeed like Tulips. They are coloured a rich lime-green with orange centres, and appear well after the foliage, often at too great a height to pick.

There are exquisite varieties with the leaves beautifully margined, though lighter areas tend to darken in late summer.

Its botanical name is **Liriodendron tulipifera** meaning the tulip-bearing lily tree. The timber is a useful, close-grained hardwood, if you could bear to cut it down.

MAGNOLIA

Magnolia denudata
Yulan

Magnolia campbellii
Chinese Tulip Tree

Yulan, Bull Bay
* **Deciduous or evergreen**/slow
* **Spring-summer**/fragrant
* **Ht: 5-50m/15-150ft**

Through a tremendous range of climates from cold temperate to subtropical, the ultimate flowering tree is a **Magnolia** of one sort or another. This is thanks to the fact that the genus has two homelands — the cold far west of China in the vicinity of the Himalayas, and southern USA and Central America on the warm gulf of Mexico.

Generally speaking, the Chinese species are deciduous and spring flowering; those from America are evergreen and bloom in summer.

The most commonly seen species in temperate climates is undoubtedly the giant American Bull Bay or Southern Magnolia, **M. grandiflora,** which may reach 25m where the winters are warm enough. It is evergreen, with very large simple leaves that look as if they have been lacquered on top and sprayed with brown flock beneath. The dinner-plate-sized flowers, with six to twelve petals, open continuously in the warm weather, spreading a rich perfume.

The deciduous Chinese species grow particularly well in acid, woodsy soil of hill areas, where one of the most commonly seen is **M. denudata,** the Yulan, a gorgeous, rounded tree that grows to 13m and produces white goblet-shaped flowers on its bare branches almost at the end of winter. These are the diameter of a saucer, and superbly perfumed.

Where you see the Yulan, you're also likely to find its hybrid **M.** X **soulangeana,** the result of a cross with **M. liliflora,** a dark purple-pink flowering species that blooms later, well after its foliage has developed. **M.** X **soulangeana** is available in a wide range of shades from almost white to almost purple. These must of course be propagated from cuttings, but are slow-growing and often seen at leggy shrub size. Given the right climate though, they can easily match the height and spread of their

Magnolia X *soulangeana*
Soulange-Bodin's Magnolia ▶

Magnolia grandiflora
Bull Bay

Magnolia veitchii
Veitch's Magnolia

Magnolia X 'Rustica Rubra'

MAGNOLIA (continued)

Yulan parent; CV 'Rustica Rubra' is a particularly vivid variety.

The giant of the family is the Chinese Tulip Tree, **M. campbellii,** reaching an unbelievable 50m in its home mountains, but so slow-growing that we have no idea of its ultimate size in cultivation. It is not likely to flower in much under twenty years, so is a real heirloom plant, but what an heirloom! Great velvety 25cm leaves, and spreading flowers of pale pink and deep rose, marvellously perfumed. Even in the autumn it is decorative, with coloured leaves and spikes of scarlet seeds. It does not like frost.

Magnolias are named for Pierre Magnol, an eighteenth century director of French botanic gardens.

Magnolia liliflora
Lily Magnolia

Malus floribunda
Japanese Crabapple

Malus ioensis
Prairie Crab

MALUS

Apple, Crabapple
* **Deciduous/fast**
* **Spring/fragrant**
* **Ht: 5-15m/15-50 ft**

If the cost of medical insurance continues to rise it may pay us to remember the old saying 'an apple a day keeps the doctor away' and plant an apple tree in our own gardens. That is, if we are prepared to take the trouble to combat such hazards as fruit fly, the codling moth and many other pests.

Alternatively, we could plant one of the many lovely varieties of flowering Crabapples or crabs, feed our souls on the beautiful spring blossom and enjoy the tangy fruit later.

From the vast number of Apples and Crabapples listed, it is hard to believe that they are all varieties of only twenty-five species. The rest are all cultivars, including over a thousand named varieties of the eating apple, **Malus domestica,** alone. Apples are all native to the temperate zone of the northern hemisphere, though they are now grown in cooler climates everywhere. They are deciduous members of the rose family, a fact which isn't surprising if you look closely at their flowers and leaves. Apple fruits are only a larger, juicier version of rose hips.

The original European Crab, **M. sylvestris,** has white flowers and is rather thorny. A reason perhaps it is not seen much in cultivation, though it is a handsome 13m tree in Europe and Asia Minor. The introduction of the Japanese Crab, **M. floribunda,** in 1862 quickly put an end to the European species' popularity. The Japanese Crab is a graceful, heavily flowering tree that scarcely reaches 8m, an ideal size for the average garden. Its buds are deep carmine, opening to rosy flowers which finally turn almost pure white. Usually all three colours are displayed at once.

The Prairie Crab, **M. ioensis,** is an American species, 10m in the wild, but often quite dwarfed in cultivation. It has rather hairy, often lobed leaves, and gorgeous semi-double pink and white flowers, rather like Cherry blossom. Each bloom is up to 5cm in diameter.

M. hupehensis is from China and grows to 8m. The leaves are long and slender, the

Malus floribunda
Japanese Crab

Malus X *purpurea* 'Eleyi'
Purple Crab

MALUS (continued)

single flowers white and the miniature red fruit on long stems are quite charming as they dangle from branch tips.

M. X **purpurea** 'Eleyi' is the Purple Crab, a decorative small tree with bronzy leaves and flowers of deep purple-pink, often variable in their colour.

Other species are grown more for the decorative effect of the fruits than for their floral display. These include the cultivars 'Gorgeous' with vivid scarlet crabs, and 'Golden Hornet' in which the fruits are orange-yellow.

Malus, the botanical name of both Apples and Crabs, is the original Roman name of the wild European species.

MELALEUCA

Paperbark, Cajeput
* **Evergreen**/**very fast**
* **Summer**/**fragrant**
* Ht: 7-20m/20-60ft

One of the best-loved Australian genera world-wide, decorative **Melaleucas** now flourish in every subtropical to temperate area of the world, often where other trees kick up their heels. There are over a hundred species, known mostly for their decorative peeling barks and colourful flower spikes on which hundreds of long-stamened flowers are arranged in the form of a bottlebrush, generally white or cream in all of the tree-sized species.

Most common is the ubiquitous **M. quinquenervia,** known as the Broadleaf Paperbark or Cajeput tree. A handsome, spreading giant growing to 25m high when planted on its own in damp ground, it is more often seen crowded in brackish swamps as a collection of slim, white-trunked saplings, with all the character of a field of clothes props. In this guise it has become unpopular in the state of Florida, where it may well succeed in taking over the famous Everglades. In contrast, the Hong Kong Government plants it widely to help stabilize swampy farming areas of the New Territories. The tree's regular display of cream bottlebrushes makes it one of the most reliable flowering trees in the world.

A second worthwhile species is decorative Snow in Summer, **M. linariifolia,** which never outgrows its welcome. Rarely above

Melaleuca quinquenervia
Cajeput Tree

7m, it has a spreading habit, inclining towards multiple trunks. This species has the spongiest, flakiest bark of all, and really does look as if a snowstorm hit it in warm weather, when all the flowers open at once.

In the Bracelet Honeymyrtle, **M. armillaris,** the leaves are modified to needleform, and the bark more furrowed than flaking. The dense flower-spikes are almost pure white and about 7.5cm long. **M. armillaris** may grow to 10m and is particularly dense-foliaged. It is often seen group-planted as a windbreak.

The West Australian **M. parviflora** really comes into its own in sandy coastal areas, where it may reach 7m. It has dark tapered leaves rarely above 1cm long, and fluffy, shorter cream bottlebrushes with an occasional dusting of red and pink.

Melaleucas are propagated from cuttings, and the botanical name is a combination of the Greek words for black and white, referring to its tonal contrasts.

Melaleuca parviflora
Paperbark

Melia azederach
Persian Lilac

MELIA

White Cedar, Persian Lilac,
Pride of India
* **Deciduous/fast**
* **Spring/fragrant**
* **Ht: to 20m/60ft** T H

Pride of India, Persian Lilac, Texas Umbrella Tree, Australian White Cedar — a partial list of names collected by the decorative **Melia azederach** serves to underline the confusion as to its original home. Today, there is hardly a country on earth where it is not known and grown.

In tropical climates it shoots up to 20m and more, with a spreading crown. In Texas, Australia and Persia it grows usually wider than its height. In all areas it bears handsome leaves that resemble those of the European Ash.

In spring, with the new foliage, **Melia** produces sprays of lilac and purple flowers, five- or six-petalled and fragrant.

Melia is of particular use in dry, semi-desert areas, though it will also withstand several degrees of frost. It is easy to propagate from seed or cuttings.

Messerschmidia argentea
Tree Heliotrope

Metrosideros kermadecensis
Variegated Ironwood

MESSERSCHMIDIA

Tree Heliotrope
* **Evergreen/fast**
* **Warm weather**
* **Ht: to 6m/20ft**

Around the Pacific and Indian Oceans (but rarely growing any great distance inland) you will find a curious, umbrella-shaped tree like a greatly enlarged bush of the popular, shrubby Heliotrope. Incredibly salt-resistant, it is **Messerschmidia argentea,** often found right at the beachline, and a great standby for coastal gardens in any warm climate. Its bark is pale and frequently deeply furrowed; the foliage clusters at the ends of windswept branches. The leaves are thick, handsome and rather like those of an avocado, though covered in silky whitish hairs. In India they are considered a delicacy, with a parsley-like flavour. Small white flowers bloom at or near the ends of the branches, frequently in broad, many-branched clusters of coiled spikes. These flower clusters persist for many months, many of them developing small, pointed green fruits. Not the most spectacular tree in the world — but for the desperate coastal gardener a great boon.

METROSIDEROS

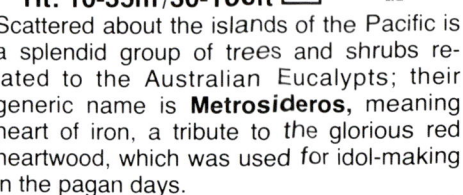

Ironwood, Pohutukawa, Rata, Ohi'a Lehua
* **Evergreen/fast**
* **Spring-summer**
* **Ht: 10-35m/30-100ft**

Scattered about the islands of the Pacific is a splendid group of trees and shrubs related to the Australian Eucalypts; their generic name is **Metrosideros,** meaning heart of iron, a tribute to the glorious red heartwood, which was used for idol-making in the pagan days.

Most splendid of all is **M. excelsa** (syn **M. tomentosa**), aptly called by the Maori Pohutukawa, or 'sprinkled with spray' for its habit of clinging to sea-washed cliffs or growing with its roots actually in salt water. It is both salt- and sand-resistant and in an exposed position will become gnarled and picturesque, trailing a tangle of aerial roots from every branch. Its dark, leathery 10cm

Metrosideros excelsa
Pohutukawa

Metrosideros robusta
Northern Rata

METROSIDEROS (continued)

leaves have silver reverses, and in midsummer (Christmas time in the southern hemisphere) it bursts into dazzling bloom as masses of scarlet-stamened pincushion flowers open on white woolly stalks.

Taller, with flowers of a duller red, is the Northern Rata, **M. robusta,** from forests of New Zealand's North Island.

A third New Zealand species, also with rounded leaves, is **M. kermadecensis,** sold in a number of variegated leaf forms.

Less useful in coastal gardens but at home in humid, mountain areas is **M. collina,** the Ohi'a Lehua, found naturally high up on the slopes of Tahiti and the Hawaiian Islands, where it has been recorded to 35m in height. Its spreading shape, crowned with a blanket of vivid red blossom, caused the Hawaiians to declare it sacred to Pele, goddess of the volcanoes.

Michelia alba
Pak-lan

Michelia champaca
Cham-pak

MICHELIA

Pak-lan, Wong-lan
Cham-pak
* **Deciduous/fast**
* **Spring/fragrant**
* **Ht: 10-30m/30-100ft**

Evergreen, and closely related to the Magnolias (which see), the fifty-odd Asiatic species of **Michelia** are commonly represented in Western gardens only by shrubby **M. figo,** the Port Wine Magnolia or Banana Shrub.

But in gardens of Asia, Hawaii, South America and Africa, several of the tree species are among the most beloved of garden ornamentals.

Three of these trees are generally available and worth seeking out. They are:

M. alba, the Pak-lan, a handsome, pale-trunked tree of 10m with slender, pointed, apple-green leaves to 25cm long. The snowy-white flowers are about the size of a Gardenia, though with narrow petals of irregular length. They are very fragrant, and a great favourite among Chinese communities everywhere. Unfortunately, they are hard to pick as the tree tends to be rather high-branching.

M. doltsopa, the Wong-lan, is a fast-growing pyramidal tree to 13m; its pointed leaves are a darker green, and the branches often develop a convenient weeping habit. The flowers are very large, often 15cm in diameter, with long, floppy petals of white, fading to a butterscotch colour. They are fragrant at first but develop an unpleasantly heavy perfume after a day.

M. champaca, the Cham-pak, is a larger-growing tree from Tibet and Yunnan. It may reach 30m in nature, but much less in the garden. The fragrant, often twelve-petalled flowers are 7.5cm wide and a creamy-buff shade.

All **Michelias** bear their flowers in the leaf axils (unlike the Magnolias).

The botanic name **Michelia** commemorates a seventeenth-century Italian botanist, Pietro Micheli.

Michelia doltsopa
Wong-lan ▶

FLOWERING TREES

Myoporum laetum
Ngaio

MYOPORUM

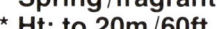

Ngaio, Boobialla
* Evergreen/slow
* Spring/fragrant
* Ht: to 20m/60ft

|T|

Asia, Australia, New Zealand and islands of the Pacific are home to more than 20 species of **Myoporum,** but few compare with Australia's slender 4m Boobialla, **M. floribundum.** A small, spreading tree, its branches are draped with fringes of dark, hanging leaves, and in spring, a frosting of white flowers that make the tree look as if it has been caught in a blizzard. It enjoys light, acid soil, as does the New Zealand Ngaio, **M. laetum,** a 5m tree with 10cm lanceolate leaves and masses of purple-spotted, white 2cm flowers, followed by red-violet fruit. Hawaii's **M. sandwicense** or Bastard Sandalwood reaches 20m in the wild. It bears white or pink flowers, and the hard, yellow-green timber is used as a sandalwood substitute.

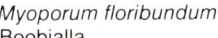

Myoporum floribundum
Boobialla

NEOLITSEA

Litsea
* **Evergreen/slow**
* **Summer/fragrant**
* **Ht: to 10m/30ft**

Somewhat resembling the European Bay Tree **(Laurus nobilis),** the Asiatic **Neolitsea** genus includes up to 150 species of both evergreen and deciduous trees, most of which can be grown in any temperate to subtropical area where the soil is well-drained, and of good quality They have some use in commerce as timber, and make decorative shade trees with handsome foliage and a mass of mildly fragrant blooms at various times of the year, according to species.

N. aciculata is a slender 4m tree with wide-ended leaves to 12.5cm in length, whitish on the reverses. Small reddish flowers are followed by black, elliptical berries. It is from Japan, as is the larger **N. sericea,** a 10m tree with a slender trunk, green branches and pointed laurel-like leaves to 17.5cm long. Young foliage is covered with yellowish hairs, but the mature leaves are a shining grey-green with silver reverses. Two sexes of flowers are borne separately on the same tree, varying only in their stamens. They are small, clustered in fragrant umbels at the leaf-axils in summer, and are followed by 5mm red fruit.

Neolitsea sericea
Litsea

FLOWERING TREES

Nuytsia floribunda
Golden Bough

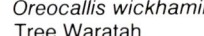
Oreocallis wickhamii
Tree Waratah

NUYTSIA

Fire Tree, Golden Bough
* **Evergreen/slow**
* **Summer**
* **Ht: to 9m/27ft** [T]

Although none of us will ever see a Fire Tree in flower unless we happen to be in West Australia around Christmas, it could not be omitted from this book.

Nuytsia floribunda is one of the most beautiful trees in the world, and it is a gigantic tree-size relative of the humble mistletoe, with no means of feeding except through the roots of established nearby host plants.

You can sow the seed, and it will sprout, but stay at seedling size for years. In nature it will send feeding stems for literally hundreds of metres in every direction, battening on every plant in sight — from grass to towering tree — and partaking delicately from each of their life support systems: a true vegetable Dracula!

OREOCALLIS

Tree Waratah, Red Silky Oak
* **Evergreen/fast**
* **Spring**
* **Ht: to 10m/30ft** [T] [H]

Much of the world seems unaware of Australia's gorgeous **Oreocallis wickhamii**, but it is quite amenable to garden use, in a position sheltered from wind and with an ample supply of moisture.

Like so many Australian natives, it is a member of the family Proteaceae, with single, tough, leathery leaves.

The flower display has brought it a number of popular names including Fire Tree, Red Silky Oak, and Tree Waratah; the latter seems most appropriate, for the inflorescence does rather resemble that of the New South Wales State floral emblem.

Oreocallis may be raised from seed, but will not commence blooming until it is reasonably adult, after about seven or eight years. In maturity it rarely exceeds 10m in height.

Oxydendrum arboreum
Sourwood

OXYDENDRUM

Sourwood, Sorrel Tree, Titi
* **Deciduous** /fast
* **Summer /autumn colour / fragrant**
* **Ht: to 7m /21ft** C T

The beautiful **Oxydendrum arboreum,** or Sourwood, from the south-east United States, resembles nothing so much as a tree-sized species of Andromeda (**Pieris** spp.). Rarely growing above 7m in cultivation, it may reach four times that height in the wild, and in both situations needs acid soil and the shelter of other larger, denser trees.

In late summer the entire tree is decked with drooping sprays of white bell-shaped blossom at branch tips, each individual flower less than 1cm long. These are delightfully fragrant, honey-rich, and most attractive to bees. The tree's special glory, however, is later in the autumn, when the deciduous foliage turns a brilliant blood-red.

Oxydendrum is easily propagated from cuttings, layers or seed.

Parkinsonia aculeata
Jerusalem Thorn

Paulownia tomentosa
Princess Tree

PARKINSONIA

Jerusalem Thorn,
Mexican Palo Verde
* **Deciduous/fast**
* **Spring/fragrant**
* **Ht: to 10m/30ft** T H

A small genus of about five trees; only one (tropical **Parkinsonia aculeata**) is much seen in cultivation, in the western United States, Hawaii and around the Mediterranean basin. It is a valuable acquisition for any garden in dry, drought-prone areas with alkaline soil balance, and grows rapidly from seed to about 4m, after which it assumes a slow, steady growth. Its bark is yellowish green, its twigs spiny, and its weeping bipinnate leaves appear most of the year as bare stems, the tiny leaflets dropping at the first sign of cold or excessive dryness. The flower display appears off and on, though most heavily in spring. It consists of 18cm clusters of sweet-scented yellow pea-flowers, marked in red. In some parts of west Australia its cultivation is prohibited.

PAULOWNIA

Princess Tree,
Mountain Jacaranda
* **Deciduous/fast** C
* **Spring/fragrant**
* **Ht: 7-13m/20-40ft** T

Named for a princess, and a true princess among trees, China's noble **Paulownias** are sometimes mistaken for the American Catalpa, and they are closely related. The principal similarity is in the green, heart-shaped, fuzzy leaves which may reach 30cm in length and almost as much across. Both tree genera bear large trumpet-shaped flowers, but those of the **Paulownia** are carried in vertical spikes. Another difference is in the seeds. Catalpa carries them in hanging pea-type pods; in **Paulownia** they are in pointed, oval capsules about 3cm across.

Paulownias flower best in a cooler-than-average climate, and will happily survive a winter minimum of −12°C/10°F, so they are most often seen in high-country gardens, where they are sometimes known as Mountain Jacaranda from their upright panicles of mauvish flowers.

P. tomentosa is the commonly seen species, reaching 13m in a good position and bearing 5cm mauve flowers, spotted violet and very fragrant. The buds appear in late summer and open in spring.

Smaller **P. fortunei** blooms earlier, rarely passes 7m. Its flowers are oyster-white marked with purple and yellow.

Paulownias are deciduous and were named for Anna Paulowna, daughter of a Russian Tsar. Propagated from seed.

Paulownia fortunei
Fortune's Paulownia

PELTOPHORUM

Yellow Poinciana,
Yellow Flame
* **Evergreen/fast**
* **Summer/fragrant**
* **Ht: to 30m/100ft** [H]

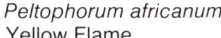

A small genus of showy, tropical shade trees, **Peltophorums** are found right around the world's tropic zone. All have lush, bipinnate leaves and fragrant golden flowers.

Illustrated **P. africanum** may grow to 13m, is decked year round with dark, shining bipinnate leaves and terminal clusters of fragrant pale-yellow blossoms that appear most heavily in summer. These are followed by brown, pea-shaped seed pods.

P. dubium is a Brazilian species in which the leaves have rusty reverses. Gold flowers appear in branched clusters and have rather wrinkled petals.

The giant of the family, found from Australia to the Philippines and Malaysia, is **P. inerme,** growing to 30m in a really tropical climate, but rarely to half that in cultivation. Its foliage is particularly heavy. The orange-yellow summer blooms open from large panicles of rusty buds at branch ends. They have a rich perfume. Altogether, marvelous specimen trees for a subtropical garden.

Peltophorum africanum
Yellow Flame

Photinia serrulata
Chinese Hawthorn

PHOTINIA

Chinese Hawthorn
* Evergreen/fast
* Spring/fragrant
* Ht: to 11m/35ft

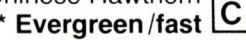

Closely related to the Hawthorns (**Crataegus,** which see), the **Photinias** are a genus of relatively small trees or large shrubs within the rose family. They come from many parts of Asia and are spectacular almost all year.

The most commonly grown is **Photinia serrulata,** popularly known as Chinese Hawthorn. It will grow anywhere in good, rich soil from either seed or cuttings, tends to push ahead fast with new growth which needs regular pruning to encourage the plant to look more like a tree.

Photinias are more often used as tall hedges or background plantings than as specimen trees. The new foliage in early spring is often highly coloured in red and orange, and is followed immediately by flat 15cm clusters of tiny, white, pungently scented blossom. Small bright red fruits follow, persisting until winter, when the tree (although evergreen) will develop some brilliant red leaf colouring. It grows well in a dry position and, its best display is seen in a cold climate.

Pittosporum daphniphylloides
Chinese Daphne

Pittosporum undulatum
Native Daphne

PITTOSPORUM

Mockorange,
Native Daphne
* **Evergreen**/fast
* **Spring/fragrant**
* **Ht: 3-13m/10-40ft**

To pronounce on which of the many **Pittosporum** species might be the most attractive would be rather like repeating the infamous Judgment of Paris. Whichever way you choose, you're bound to engender jealousy somewhere, for national feelings tend to run high in such matters. Let me say merely that the **Pittosporum** are a genus of about seventy-five handsome evergreens with flowers fragrant as orange blossom.

All of them are found in an area centring on Australia, but with outlying species in east Africa, Japan, South-East Asia, New Zealand and Hawaii.

New Zealand's big entry in the contest is

Pittosporum phillyraeoides
Willow Pittosporum

PITTOSPORUM (continued)

blonde: **P. eugenioides variegatum,** a striking tree with cream-margined grey-green leaves, greenish-yellow flowers and a height of 13m. It is known locally as the Silver Tarata.

Japan throws into the ring the universally popular **P. tobira** or Mockorange, a 7m shrubby tree with fragrant cream blossom and bright yellow seed capsules.

Australia has two main contenders: the Willow Pittosporum **(P. phillyraeoides),** a slender, willowy weeping-branched tree of 10m with yellow flowers in axillary clusters. Its companion, **P. undulatum,** the Victorian Box or Native Daphne, grows taller, has pointed leaves of a distinctive pale green, and creamy-white blossom in 7.5cm terminal bunches.

Across the seas in Taiwan is a rank outsider, the small 3m **P. daphnipylloides,** which bears masses of tiny, fragrant golden flowers at the end of branchlets.

Hawaii loves the Ho'awa **(P. hosmeri),** a small tree with wonderfully wrinkled leaves and fragrant cream flowers.

I'll leave it to someone else to make the judgment between them, and in a cowardly fashion just suggest that though they are all beautiful, they are best kept away from paths. Their sticky fruits get on everyone's feet and into everybody's favourite carpet.

Needless to say, all **Pittosporums** grow easily from seed.

Plumeria acuminata
'Common Yellow' Frangipani ▶

P. 125

PLUMERIA

Frangipani, Graveyard Tree, Temple Flower
* **Deciduous**/fast
* **Warm weather**/fragrant
* **Ht: 8-15m/24-45ft**

|T| |H|

While it is often found planted about Asian temples and burial grounds, there is nothing really sinister in the **Plumeria's** common name of Graveyard Tree. It has been honoured by the Buddhists for centuries as a symbol of immortality, and in Sri Lanka is sometimes known as the Tree of Life.

Both of these popular epithets are due to its ability to continue flowering even when not in the ground, as any gardener who has ever forgotten to plant a large cutting can testify.

Though seen throughout the warm climates of the world, all **Plumerias** were originally native to central America and carried to the East by Spanish traders.

Modern research suggests the myriad colour varieties are all hybrids among five recognised species.

These species are: **P. acuminata** — cream and yellow flowers, pale pointed leaves; **P. alba** — small white and yellow flowers, paddle-shaped leaves; **P. bahamensis** — white flowers, narrow, dark leaves; **P. obtusa** — large, rounded white flowers, dark, evergreen leaves with rounded tips; and **P. rubra** — red flowers, shorter, rounded leaves.

In really tropical areas they grow into quite large trees. I have seen them in the Philippines to 13m in height and with a trunk as thick as a barrel.

Plumerias grow readily from cuttings of any size, thoroughly dried out before planting. They can also be raised from seed, though the colour of the resulting flowers would be anybody's guess.

In tropical climates the richly fragrant flower clusters appear directly from the bare, winter branches, and continue to open all year. In more temperate zones, the new foliage appears first and flowering does not begin till late spring.

Plumerias were named for Charles Plumier, a seventeenth century French botanical writer. In many lands they are called Frangipani.

Plumeria X 'Scott Pratt'

Plumeria obtusa
Singapore White Plumeria

◀ *Plumeria acuminata* hybrid

FLOWERING TREES

Pomaderris apetala
Tainui

POMADERRIS

Tainui, Native Hazel
* Evergreen/fast
* Spring
* Ht: to 5m/15ft   [T]

Native to both Australia and New Zealand, the decorative **Pomaderris apetala** is also popular in California, where it seems to grow better than in its natural range. It is a fast-growing, slender tree with all parts except the trunk covered in greyish down. The 10cm leaves, often with a wrinkled surface, are dark and handsome. The tiny white or yellow flowers have no petals, but consist of stamens, borne in woolly masses to 20cm in diameter. They persist for months. **Pomaderris** can be struck from well-ripened cuttings, does best in a moist, sheltered position.

Posoqueria latifolia
Needle-flower Tree

POSOQUERIA

Needle-flower Tree
* Evergreen/fast   [T]
* Spring/fragrant
* Ht: to 7m/20ft   [H]

Rivalling the perfume of the Frangipani in gardens of warm climates is the exotic Needle-flower Tree, **Posoqueria latifolia,** whose white blossoms open throughout the spring season.

It reaches tree size only in hot climates, but is decorative any place you find it, with brilliantly glossy 20cm evergreen leaves putting on a show at all times.

The flowers are really extraordinary: 15cm long tubes tipped with pointed buds that spring open as dainty white reflexed flowers, sometimes with projecting anthers. These appear in densely-crowded clusters at branch tips, and continue to open for months. Occasional yellow, plum-sized fruits are edible, but rarely appetizing.

Posoqueria is normally propagated from cuttings, and grows rapidly in the deep rich soil it likes. It is hardy down to about −3°C/27°F.

Prunus persica
Flowering Peach

Prunus X *blireiana*
Purple-leafed Plum

PRUNUS

Flowering Peaches, Plums, Cherries and Apricots
 * **Deciduous/fast**
 * **Winter-spring/fragrant**
 * **Ht: 7-20m/21-65ft**   [C]   [T]

'Roses by many other names' might be the simplest way to describe the hundreds of **Prunus** species in a single sentence. For they are members of the Rose family, and they do all bear flowers with a passing resemblance to roses. But beyond that it takes a really creative imagination to spot the relationship between, say, a flowering Cherry **(P. serrulata)** and an evergreen Cherry Laurel **(P. laurocerasus)**.

For horticultural purposes, one has to make an artificial division of this very large genus — over 200 species and probably upwards of 2000 cultivars — all of them from the northern hemisphere.

That division is between the species grown for the delight of the appetite, and the others grown purely for eye appeal. To take them in that order, the popular edible

130 • FLOWERING TREES

Prunus campanulata
Taiwan Cherry

PRUNUS (continued)

species include: the Apricot, **Prunus armeniaca;** the Cherry, **P. cerasus;** the Plum, **P. domestica;** the Almond, **P. dulcis;** the Peach, **P. persica,** together with a host of minor species with local flavour appeal — the American Red Plum, **P. americana;** the Gean, **P. avium;** the Cherry Plum, **P. cerasifera;** the Goose Plum, **P. hortulana;** the Greengages and Damsons, **P. institia;** the St Lucie Cherry, **P. mahaleb;** the Japanese Plum, **P. salicina;** the Sloe, **P. spinosa;** the Nanking Cherry, **P. tomentosa;** and the Almond Cherry, **P. triloba.**

Most of these are to one degree or another bushy trees, rarely above 7m; they need a deal of pruning or shaping to produce a satisfactory fruit crop. All are deciduous, with attractive, single rose-type flowers in early spring, either pale pink or white. These appear generally on small spur-like branchlets designed to take the

Prunus mume
Flowering Apricot

Prunus serrulata 'Kanzan'
Flowering Cherry

Prunus serrulata 'Shirotae'
Mt Fuji Cherry

Prunus serrulata 'Shimidsu Sakura'
Flowering Cherry

Prunus serrulata 'Ukon'
Green Cherry

132 • FLOWERING TREES

Prunus subhirtella
Rosebud Cherry

Prunus subhirtella pendula
Weeping Cherry

PRUNUS (continued)

weight of the fruit. All fruiting species may be grown from their seeds or stones, but are generally propagated by bud grafting to be certain of variety and quality.

By far the most popular group of ornamentals are the Japanese Flowering Cherries, mostly hybrids of **P. serrulata** with a number of other oriental species. These have flowers both single and double, in a wide range of colours from pure white to deep red, sometimes with variegation. Often the individual flowers are borne on long, hanging stems. In their home country of Japan, their cultivation is a way of life, and springtime Cherry Blossom viewing an annual event to which everyone looks forward.

Another popular species is the Weeping or Rosebud Cherry, **P. subhirtella pendula,** whose delightful miniature blossoms may appear in autumn as well as spring. This is a great favourite, together with the Taiwan Cherry, **P. campanulata,** whose delicate trumpet-shaped red blossom is among the earliest to open in spring.

Less often seen away from its native China and Japan is **P. mume,** the Japanese Flowering Apricot or Plum. This is usually the first to bloom, often in mid-winter, and has almost as many attractive cultivars as the cherry. The flowers are generally flat and open, with a spectacular display of stamens, and may be in any colour from white to deep red.

In Western gardens, the spring display is provided more by a range of hybrid flowering peaches, including cultivars of **P. amygdalus,** the Flowering Almond, **P. persica,** the Peach, and many other minor species. These include ornamental varieties of **P. avium** which may grow to 23m, **P. X blireiana,** the Purple-leafed Plum with single pink flowers, and the similar **P. pissardii.**

Finally, there are several less common evergreen species grown as much for the beauty of their foliage as for their generally white blossom. They are sometimes pruned as hedges, or certain low-growing species are used as ground covers. The evergreen types include the Californian **P. ilicifolia;** the Versailles or Cherry Laurel, **P. laurocerasus;** and the Portugal Laurel, **P. lusitanica;** all of these are small growing.

Pterocarya fraxinifolia
Caucasian Wingnut

Pterospermum acerifolium
Bayur Tree

PTEROCARYA

Caucasian Wingnut
* **Deciduous/fast**
* **Summer**
* **Ht: to 35m/100ft**

C T

The dangling golden catkins of **Pterocarya** put one more in mind of a Wistaria than a Walnut, yet they are related to the latter.

The genus is found exclusively in Asia — ten species from the Caucasus to China, all big growers to 30m and more. They are particularly beautiful near water, where their appearance is lush and tropical. Yet they are deciduous and perfectly suited to a wide range of temperate climates.

Pterocarya fraxinifolia, the Caucasian Wingnut, is the only species seen much outside its native range.

PTEROSPERMUM

Bayur Tree
* **Deciduous/fast**
* **Summer/fragrant**
* **Ht: to 35m/100ft**

T H

The Bayur (its botanical name is **Pterospermum acerifolium**) is among the world's most spectacular tropical trees, native to India and Indonesia, yet flowering just as well in a warm temperate climate. It grows to 35m in the wild, but mercifully much smaller in the garden. Its attractive leaves are the size and shape of a rather wilted dinner plate, and in summer the flower buds develop both at leaf axils and in small terminal clusters. They are like large

FLOWERING TREES

Pyrus pashia
Indian Pear

Pyrus communis
Common or Wild Pear

PTEROSPERMUM (continued)

cigars, and you're most unlikely to see one opening, for that happens at night. The morning after, the cigar is seen to have split into five richly-cream reflexed petals, and in the centre is revealed a 15cm fountain of white, fragrant stamens.

PYRUS

Pear
* **Deciduous/slow**
* **Spring/fragrant**
* **Ht: to 20m/60ft** C T

We all believe blind Freddie could tell the difference between an apple and a pear and we would probably all be wrong. For until recent times many trees we now know as Quince, Medlar and Crabapple were classed, with many others, as Pears, or botanically as **Pyrus** species.

Pear fruits, for instance, are not necessarily 'pear-shaped'. Sometimes they are round, sometimes flattened like a tomato. They have a different structure to apples though. Their stalks are thicker and do not join onto the fruit in a hollow. They are sort-of streamlined in.

Their flowers are similar to apple blossom, which is to say, like white, single roses, and they are as showy in the garden as any ornamental blossom tree.

The leaves of some Pear species are rounder and shinier than those of an apple, more like a Poplar's perhaps. But not all species. The foliage of **P. salicifolia,** the lovely Willow-leaf Pear from Asia Minor, is long, greyish and covered all over with silver-silky hair. With its tight, flat heads of snowy blossom, it would make a splendid feature for an all-white garden.

The Indian Pear, **P. pashia,** has toothed dark leaves and is quite colourful in bloom, with pink buds and white blossom.

The European Wild Pear, **P. communis,** is the ancestor of all the Pears we grow for the table. It has varieties with fruits of many colours, and the single flowers may be white or pink, generally with a rather acrid perfume. They grow quite large, albeit slowly. I have seen them 20m and more in old European gardens.

Rhodoleia championii
Silk Rose

RHODOLEIA

Silk Rose, Champara
* Evergreen/fast
* Spring/fragrant
* Ht: to 10m/30ft

Not really common anywhere, even in its native South China, the Silk Rose, **Rhodoleia championii,** was first discovered only in 1849. But it has been distributed to all continents by garden connoisseurs and is worth seeking out as a medium-sized specimen tree for sheltered gardens. Given the protection of other, larger trees, it will reach 10m and flower heavily when quite young.

A leggy, sparsely branched plant, it greatly resembles some of the larger **Rhododendrons** in habit, but is not related to them, rather to the Witch-hazels (**Hamamelis** spp.).

The dark, leathery, oblong leaves are perfectly smooth above, greyish beneath, and crowd at the end of branchlets like those of **Tristania** (which see). The spring flowers appear in heads of five to ten, from leaf axils near the branch tips, each a wide, hanging bell of purest carmine, about 4cm in diameter.

Each **Rhodoleia** blossom is actually a group of five flowers, surrounded by a common row of petals.

Rhodoleia (from the Greek **rhodon** meaning 'rose' and **leios** meaning 'smooth') enjoys humidity, part sun and deep acid soil.

It is propagated from ripened cuttings, and the new foliage buds appear in whorls about a central leading shoot on each branch.

Robinia pseudacacia
Black Locust

Robinia X 'Bella Rosea'

ROBINIA

Black Locust Tree
* **Deciduous/fast**
* **Spring/fragrant**
* **Ht: to 25m/80ft**

As American as Apple Pie, all twenty species of the genus **Robinia** occur naturally within the mainland of the United States, though they have long since spread over the border in both directions, even over surrounding oceans to become naturalized in Australia, southern Europe and many other places.

They are generally spiny members of the Pea family, Leguminosae, and like so many of their relatives bear fragrant pea-type flowers, and dangling pea-type pods. It was the pods in fact, that led to the popular name of Black Locust, as early colonists found they resembled those of the related Locust Tree of southern Europe **(Ceratonia)**. The name **Robinia** celebrates Jean Robin, a royal herbalist who first grew the trees in Paris about 1600.

The commonly seen and frequently naturalized species is **R. pseudacacia,** from central North America. It is a tall tree growing to 25m, with dark gnarled trunk and frequently picturesque branches. Its deciduous leaves have many leaflets and are a handsome light green.

For garden usage, many attractive cultivars have been developed from it, including: CV 'Fastigiata', with a tall, poplar-like shape; CV 'Tortuosa', whose branches are layered and twisted like an intricately trained Japanese bonsai; CV 'Inermis', which blessedly has no spines, but alas, precious few flowers either; and the gorgeous CV 'Frisia', which has scarlet spines and foliage of an almost fluorescent golden green. This cultivar is quite stunning when backlit by a rising or setting sun.

Foliage of all **Robinia** species turns a pale gold before leaf fall. They are easily propagated from seed or suckers, but, of course, the fancy varieties must be grafted.

Several less commonly seen species produce flowers in various shades of pink. They too have crossed with **R. pseudacacia** to produce rose-flowered cultivars such as the illustrated **R. X ambigua** 'Bella Rosea'.

Rothmannia globosa
Tree Gardenia

ROTHMANNIA

Tree Gardenia
* **Semi-deciduous/ slow**
* **Spring/fragrant**
* **Ht: to 7m/20ft**

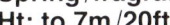

Known for many years as **Gardenia globosa,** and still sometimes sold under that name, **Rothmannia globosa** (together with several other Gardenias) has been switched to a new generic name, but are, for all that, no less fragrant or desirable specimens for the home garden.

The **Rothmannias** (now 20 species of them) are small, lightweight trees with almost black branches and shining Gardenia-type leaves to 15cm in length. Like true Gardenias, they enjoy acid soil, plenty of water and regular feeding with an acid-based fertilizer or manure. The blooms are quite different to those of the shrubby Gardenias, being bell-shaped. In the most popular **Rothmannia globosa** they are creamy-white in colour, borne in clusters at branch ends and leaf axils. Each bloom is broadly tubular, about 5cm in length, with round-pointed petals folded outward, revealing a series of pink lines decorating the open throat. The tree often becomes partly deciduous at flowering time, and blooms are followed by woody, dark brown seed capsules 2cm wide.

SARACA

Asoka
* **Deciduous/fast**
* **Dry season/fragrant**
* **Ht: to 10m/30ft**

Saracas are among the most spectacular flowering trees for subtropical gardens — particularly at the beginning and end of the tropical dry season. The flowers open a pale orange, turn red within a couple of days, presenting a razzle-dazzle of gold and purple stamens.

Though a large tree in its native jungles of South-East Asia, **Saraca indica** remains a manageable 7m in cultivation. It enjoys a humid atmosphere and rich soil.

The colour display is greatly admired in Florida, Hawaii, the Philippines and northern Australia.

In India, **Saraca** is called Asoka; Buddha is said to have been born under one.

S. declinata is almost identical, but with longer leaf stems. **S. thaipingensis** produces yellow blossom.

Saraca indica
Asoka

Saraca thaipingensis

SCHEFFLERA

(No popular name)
* Evergreen/fast
* Winter
* Ht: to 5m/15ft

T H

All greatly resembling **Brassaia** (which see), **Schefferas** include some 150 small trees and tall shrubs widely distributed in the tropics. Many of them are grown as house plants, others are valued for dense tropical effect in the warm-climate garden. Generally they have compound leaves with leaflets spread like the fingers of a hand, and bear large clusters of small flowers in racemes, panicles or umbels. Among the best known are: New Zealand's **S. digitata,** which has thin, toothed leaflets and green flowers; Java's **S. polybotrya,** with warty branches, 20cm pointed leaflets in groups of 5 to 7, and greenish Aralia-type flowers borne in red-stemmed racemes in the cooler months. These are followed by peppercorn-size fruits.

Schefflera polybotrya

SCHIZOLOBIUM

Yellow Jacaranda,
Bacurubu
* **Deciduous/fast**
* **Late spring/fragrant**
* **Ht: to 40m/130ft**

H

Towering 40m in the air, like a gigantic tree fern, the beautiful Brazilian Bacurubu is outstanding, even in a country noted for its magnificent trees.

But in subtropical gardens of Queensland, Florida, the Philippines and other warm places, the effect is unbelievable, particularly when planted in conjunction with Jacarandas and Erythrinas.

The Bacurubu (botanically **Schizolobium parahybum**) is a fragrant member of the pea family. Sparsely branched, it sprouts the largest compound leaves in the world, up to 2m in length. In spring these droop and fall, just before the branch tips sprout 30cm spikes of vivid yellow blossom.

The flowers are followed by pods, each containing one seed for propagation.

Schizolobium parahybum
Yellow Jacaranda

Sesbania grandiflora
Vegetable Humming Bird

SESBANIA

Vegetable Humming Bird
* **Evergreen/fast**
* **Wet, warm weather**
* **Ht: to 8m/25ft**

From Australia's tropical far north all the way through the Malaysian area to India, you'll find an untidy and fast-growing tropical tree often naturalized in dense groves.

Sesbania grandiflora is its botanical name, but it is more often known as Corkwood, for its fast growth goes hand-in-hand with a poor, weak constitution and a tendency to frequent splitting and short life.

Though not popular in cultivation due to this inherent weakness, it makes an acceptable specimen in warm-climate gardens until more permanent trees can grow sufficiently to take its place.

It is a member of the vast Pea family, Leguminosae, with soft green compound leaves of up to sixty leaflets, and a height rarely exceeding 8m. Throughout the warm months, particularly following a wet spell, remarkably handsome flowers appear at the leaf-axils, from which they hang like feeding birds.

The flowers are followed by long, flat seed pods, and the leaves, flowers and young pods are all edible.

Sesbania is an approximation of the tree's name in Arabic.

SOLANUM

Potato Tree
* **Evergreen/fast**
* **Spring/fragrant**
* **Ht: to 5m/15ft**

A tree-size shrub or a shrubby tree — who can tell which? But this spectacular Brazilian plant makes a great show in warm-climate or tropical gardens, blooming throughout the warmer weather. **Solanum macranthum** grows normally with a single trunk, the branches covered thickly with striking 10-lobed 38cm leaves that are quite prickly along well delineated veins. The bluish-violet flowers (to 7cm in diameter) appear in racemes of 7-12 blooms. Except for the colour, they are identical to those of the potato or eggplant, both of which are closely related.

SOPHORA

Kowhai, Pagoda Tree, Frijolito
* **Deciduous/fast**
* **Spring-summer/ fragrant**
* **Ht: 13-27m/40-80ft**

Scattered all about the mighty Pacific, a genus of the Pea family named **Sophora** is found in Japan, Korea, New Zealand, Chile, Hawaii and the south-west United States. Fairly typical members of the Pea family, they are generally frost-hardy, and with a capacity for display rivalling the European Laburnums.

First discovered and still the most popular is the Japanese Pagoda Tree **(S. japonica),** a widely used species for street planting in Europe, Japan and parts of the United States. It is a tall grower, to 27m high, but often kept pruned to a more reasonable size. The deciduous foliage is dense, made up of a number of compound leaves with up to seventeen small leaflets each. The tiny pea flowers are cream, fragrant, and frost the entire tree in summer.

There is a charming variety **S. j. pendula,** with stiffly weeping branches.

In both New Zealand and Chile you'll find the Kowhai, **S. tetraptera.** This is much

Solanum macranthum
Potato Tree

Sophora secundiflora
Frijolito

FLOWERING TREES

SOPHORA (continued)

Sophora japonica
Pagoda Tree

smaller, rarely above 5m, and evergreen when young. It has compound leaves with up to eighty leaflets, borne sparsely on zig-zag branchlets. Many leaflets drop in spring, just before the flowers open — 7cm golden pea blossoms that droop in clusters of four to eight.

Kowhai is the tree's Maori name, and it has been selected as New Zealand's national tree.

A similar species, **S. chrysophylla,** the Mamane, is found at high altitudes in the Hawaiian Isles, while the south-west United States has a native species **S. secundiflora** with violet-scented mauve blossom.

All species of **Sophora** can be propagated from seed or cuttings, do best in a mild-temperate climate.

Sophora tetraptera
Kowhai

Spathodea campanulata
African Tulip Tree

Spathodea campanulata

SPATHODEA

African Tulip Tree,
Baton du Sorcier
* **Evergreen/fast**
* **Hot weather**
* **Ht: to 17m/50ft**

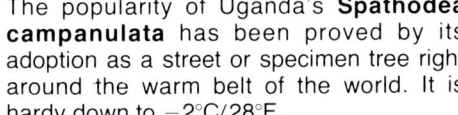

The popularity of Uganda's **Spathodea campanulata** has been proved by its adoption as a street or specimen tree right around the warm belt of the world. It is hardy down to −2°C/28°F.

Easy to propagate from seed, **Spathodea** grows to 17m in the wild. The leaves are large, ruffled and compound.

Flowers are a vivid orange-scarlet lined with yellow and may be 10cm in diameter. They appear in large clusters at the ends of branches, the display lasting months.

Spathodea goes by many popular names in many lands, and is seen blazing away in southern USA, the Caribbean, eastern Australia and Hong Kong.

144 • FLOWERING TREES

Stemmadenia galleotteana
Lecheso

STEMMADENIA

Lecheso
* **Evergreen/fast**
* **Spring-summer/ fragrant**
* **Ht: to 7m/20ft**

In its native Central America, the sap of **Stemmadenia galleotteana** is said to be poisonous, but that does not reduce its popularity in tropical gardens. Somewhat pyramidal in shape when young, the tree then develops a spreading habit, never growing very large. It is related to the Frangipani, and can easily be mistaken for one at a distance. The glossy, pointed-oval leaves appear in pairs — each leaf about 12.5cm in length. The white, crepe-like flowers look rather like those of an Oleander, and may appear at any time during the warmer months. They are 7.5cm wide, pure white with a yellow throat and the five broad overlapping petals have a pleated effect around the edges. These are followed by paired 1cm orange-red fruits.

Related **S. glabra** is very similar, but with larger leaves and pale yellow flowers.

Stenocarpus sinuatus
Wheel of Fire

STENOCARPUS

Firewheel Tree,
Wheel of Fire
* **Evergreen/slow**
* **Late summer-autumn**
* **Ht: to 35m/100ft**

Australian in origin, the gorgeous Queensland Firewheel Tree seems more appreciated in California, where they have planted some stunning avenues of them.

Stenocarpus sinuatus (meaning 'narrow fruit with wavy foliage') may reach 30m in its native forests, but rarely half that in cultivation. It needs protection from frost when young, grows slowly to a splendid vertical shape, reminiscent of a Lombardy Poplar. The dark, glossy leaves with sinuate edges may reach 25cm in length, and the flowers appear in long-stalked clusters right out of the trunk or larger branches. At first green, they develop a unique wheel shape before they turn a glowing red. Finally, each series of flowers

S. 145

Stenocarpus sinuatus
Firewheel Tree

(the spokes of the wheel) splits open to reveal the golden stamens, when the whole flower takes on the appearance of a medieval crown. The warmer the climate, the more heavily the flowers are borne, generally around early autumn.

Stenocarpus is a member of the family Proteaceae, which includes a large number of Australian trees, among them **Buckinghamia, Macadamia** and **Oreocallis.**

Stewartia pseudocamellia
Japanese Stewartia

STEWARTIA

Japanese Stewartia
* **Deciduous/slow** [C]
* **Summer/fragrant** [T]
* **Ht: to 16m/50ft**

A charming group of deciduous trees related to the Camellia, **Stewartias** are found both in Asia and in eastern North America. The Camellia-like flowers appear singly in axils of the lightly-toothed leaves. **Stewartias** are fussy about soil, preferring one that is well drained, yet acid and peaty. They resent root disturbance, must be planted quite small in a partly shaded position.

Japanese **S. pseudocamellia** is the best-known species, growing in cultivation to less than its natural 16m height. The flowers are white, with slightly ragged petal edges and brilliant orange-yellow stamens. **Stewartias** show brilliant autumn leaf-colouring: purple, orange and yellow.

Syncarpia glomulifera
Turpentine

SYNCARPIA

Turpentine
* **Evergreen/fast**   [C]
* **Spring/fragrant** [T] [H]
* **Ht: to 25m/86ft**

Possibly the finest and most useful tree of Australia's east coast is the Turpentine, **Syncarpia glomulifera,** found abundantly in southern New South Wales. Often mistaken for a Eucalypt (to which it is related), the Turpentine sends up a towering trunk as high as 25m. This is particularly sought-after for underwater construction. It is completely resistant to toredo and other marine borers due to impregnation with a turpentine-scented resin.

The Turpentine's dark 9cm leaves are tough and wavy, with silvery-grey reverses. Like Eucalyptus blossom, the creamy white flowers are a mass of stamens and appear each spring. The big difference is they occur generally seven at a time, fused together on long stalks.

Syncarpia is grown widely in the southern United States and Hawaii, as a shade and timber tree.

There is one other tree in the genus, larger-leafed **S. hillii,** the Peebeen, found only on Queensland's Fraser Island.

SYZYGIUM

Lillypilly, Rose Apple,
* **Evergreen/fast**
* **Summer/fragrant**
* **Ht: 10-27m/30-80ft**

A taxonomist's nightmare and a great nuisance to gardeners, these lovely trees have changed names as often as Elizabeth Taylor: **Acmena, Phyllocladyx, Eugenia, Myrtus** and now — **Syzygium!**

The *latest* division has all species of **Eugenia** from the Old World (Africa, Asia, Australia) classed as **Syzygium** for reasons involving the seeds. But they are still labelled **Eugenia** in most of the world's major botanic gardens.

There are between four and five hundred of them, all with glossy, evergreen foliage, often brilliantly coloured when new. Flowers are creamy-white or pink, a mass of stamens, and very attractive to bees. In all the principal species, the flowers are followed by vividly coloured fruits. They like warm-temperate to tropical climates, enjoy humidity; not resistant to frost when young.

Among the popularly grown species are:

S. aromaticum, the Clove, from the Moluccas, has clove-scented leaves and its buds are the cloves in your kitchen.

S. coolminianum, the Blue Lillypilly, from Australia.

S. grande, the Sea Apple, from Thailand.

S. jambos, the Rose Apple or Jumbu; this is the golden fruit of immortality in Buddhist legends.

S. floribundum, the Weeping Myrtle, from Australia.

S. luehmannii, the Cherry Alder or Water Myrtle, Australian.

S. malaccense, the lovely Malay Apple, with purple-pink flowers.

S. paniculatum, Brush Cherry, Australian. Most of the above are cultivated as specimen trees in warm-climate gardens throughout the world.

But **Syzygium?** I looked it up in my trusty *Funk and Wagnalls* and all that tells me is that a **syzygy** is the point of conjunction of two heavenly bodies. The connection eludes me, but the word is a sure winner for my next game of scrabble.

Syzygium jambos
Rose Apple

Syzygium malaccense
Malay Apple

FLOWERING TREES

Tabebuia chrysantha
Golden Trumpet Tree

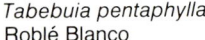

Tabebuia pentaphylla
Roblé Blanco

TABEBUIA

Trumpet Tree, Roblé Blanco
* **Deciduous/fast**
* **Winter-spring**
* **Ht: 7-27m/20-80ft** [T] [H]

Among the most beautiful of flowering trees for warmer climates are the **Tabebuias,** all from the tropical Americas and bearing the same spectacular trumpet flowers as the climbing Bignonias to which they are related. They grow rapidly in deep, rich soil and flower while quite young.

Among the best are:

T. chrysantha, the Golden Trumpet Tree, whose vivid yellow blossom opens irregularly over a long period, beginning at the end of winter.

T. pentaphylla, known variously as the Rosy Trumpet Tree, Roblé Blanco and White Cedar, bears rosy trumpet flowers in profusion at many times of the year.

TAMARIX

Flowering Cypress,
Tamarisk, Salt Cedar
* **Deciduous/fast**
* **Spring-summer/
fragrant**
* **Ht: to 10m/30ft**

C T H

Hard to believe any plant as graceful as a Tamarisk could be so incredibly tough! The feathery branchlets of minute pink blossom move in the slightest breeze, yet the same trees thrive in howling coastal gales and salt-laden soil! They are best grown from 2cm thick cuttings set in their final position and watered well. They do not transplant well due to very long tap roots. **Tamarix parviflora** from south-east Europe has almost invisible scale-like leaves on long arching stems. Prune back in winter, for it flowers best on new growth. Similar **T. pentandra** blossoms in summer.

Tamarix parviflora
Flowering Cypress

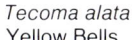

Tecoma alata
Yellow Bells

TECOMA

Yellow Bells, Yellow Elder
* **Evergreen/fast**
* **Summer/fragrant**
* **Ht: to 7m/20ft**

T H

Clustered bells of vivid yellow set off to perfection by a background of crepy green foliage. That is what identifies the brilliant Yellow Elder, **Tecoma stans,** a useful, though sparsely-furnished small tree for mild-winter areas. Its leaves are composed of five or seven deeply veined, sharply pointed and toothed leaflets, while in summer, every branch is tipped with a large panicle of 50 or more 3cm golden bell-flowers. These are 5cm long, 4cm wide, with orange stripes marking the throat. They are very fragrant, attracting bees and (if they are native to your area), humming birds. Mexico is their native territory — spreading to Peru and some Caribbean Islands. Related **T. alata** flowers in a richer yellow, often tinged orange — and its tubular flower buds may be quite red. It is probably a natural hybrid.

Thevetia yccotli
Yellow Oleander

THEVETIA

Yellow Oleander,
Be-Still Tree
* **Evergreen/fast**
* **Spring-summer/ fragrant**
* **Ht: 5-10m/15-30ft**

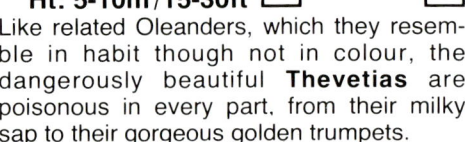

Like related Oleanders, which they resemble in habit though not in colour, the dangerously beautiful **Thevetias** are poisonous in every part, from their milky sap to their gorgeous golden trumpets.

The most commonly seen is **T. peruviana,** sometimes called Be-Still Tree, from the constant air movement of its spidery, short-stemmed leaves. It grows to 10m in height, bears lightly-fragrant 5cm golden trumpet flowers, followed by angular red fruits which ripen black. Its variety **aurantiaca** has salmon-orange flowers.

Closely related **T. thevetioides** bears much larger, more open flowers of a clearer yellow.

A third species **T. yccotli** (also from Mexico) has slightly hairy reverses to the leaves.

Thevetias can be propagated from seed or cuttings and enjoy a sandy soil.

Thevetia peruviana
Be-Still Tree

Thevetia thevetioides
Yellow Oleander

Tipuana tipu
Pride of Bolivia

TIPUANA

Pride of Bolivia
 * **Deciduous/fast**
 * **Spring**
 * **Ht: to 30m/100ft**

Found principally in mountainous Bolivia, the showy **Tipuana tipu** (an adaptation of its Indian name) has become a favourite shade tree in Mediterranean areas.

It is an untypical member of the Pea family, Leguminosae, and the only one of its genus. **Tipuana** is a tall, slender grower, 30m or more in its native forests, but fortunately remains a more manageable size in cultivation. After a rather slow beginning it tends to develop a feathery, spreading crown.

Tipuana is deciduous, producing a fresh crop of rich green leaves together with its flower display in late spring. The leaves are compound, with up to eleven pairs of leaflets, and the brilliant orange-yellow blossoms are open in shape. They appear in long sprays at branch tips, and are followed by large winged seeds.

In subtropical climates, the tree is bare for only a short period. Its accepted popular name is Pride of Bolivia.

In the grand days of Victorian cabinet-making, its wood was often sold (together with that of other trees) as Brazilian Rosewood.

Tristania laurina
Kanooka

Tristania conferta
Brush Box

TRISTANIA

Water Gum, Brush Box
* **Evergreen/fast**
* **Late spring/fragrant**
* **Ht: 20-40m/60-120ft**

Named for an all-but-forgotten French botanist, Jules Tristan, the handsome **Tristanias** are a small genus found in Australia, New Caledonia and India. Only four are of any interest to the gardener, by far the most important being the Australian Brush Box, **Tristania conferta.**

A good-natured giant with lofty, reddish trunk and branches, it may reach 40m in a warm, moist climate, but is rather prone to frost damage when young.

The glossy, simple leaves may reach 15cm and are carried alternately. The flowers, borne profusely among new foliage at the branch tips in late spring, are creamy-white, five-petalled and fragrant, with masses of feathery stamens. They are followed by round seed pods that hang on the branches all year, looking rather like the gumnuts borne by related Eucalypts.

Although **Tristania** is native to moist coastal forests and grows fast when young, it is surprisingly resistant to dry conditions, and has become very popular as a street tree in Australian cities. There, in a lopped, spreading shape, it is only a shadow of its tall free-growing forest cousins. There is a beautifully variegated form, **T. c. aurea variegata,** most eye-catching against a dark background.

Second in popularity is the Australian Water Gum or Kanooka, **T. laurina.** This is a much smaller tree, rarely 20m in nature, usually about 5m in cultivation. Similar in most respects to the Brush Box, its leaves are narrower and darker; the smaller flowers are noted for their brilliant golden colour rather than their fragrance. As its popular name suggests, it is a water-loving tree, and found wild along damp river banks.

Since this book was first published, taxonomists have been busy. The only remaining **Tristania** is a shrub. **T. conferta** (illustrated) has been rechristened **Lophostemon confertus,** while related **T. laurina** and **T. neriifolia** comprise a new genus, **Tristaniopsis.**

Brush Box timber is a popular hardwood for many home building projects.

TUPIDANTHUS

Mallet Flower
* **Evergreen/fast**
* **Summer**
* **Ht: to 7m/20ft**

Never was a popular name more apt than for the curious inflorescence of this remarkable tree. The flowers are greenish, hemispherical with 50-70 white stamens arranged around the perimeter. They develop in angular long-stemmed clusters, hidden by the foliage. The young tree may be slender with multiple trunks, but if side trunks are removed, the remaining one will expand to a squat, grotesque appearance with warty bark that extends onto the heavy branches. **Tupidanthus calyptratus** is easily propagated from cuttings, and is cultivated principally for its striking, compound leaves, each consisting of 7-9 long drooping leaflets. In its native area from India to Kampuchea, **Tupidanthus** sometimes goes berserk, turning into a heavy climber that has wrecked many ancient buildings.

Tupidanthus calyptratus
Mallet Flower

TUTCHERIA

(No common name)
* **Evergreen/fast**
* **Summer/fragrant**
* **Ht: to 10m/30ft**

Several species of **Tutcheria** are native to south-east China and closely related to the Camellia. Pyramidal when young, the trees develop a spreading shape at maturity, being covered at all times with long-pointed, glossy 15cm leaves. These are distinctly V-shaped in section and lightly serrated. Young growth of **Tutcheria spectabilis** is reddish in colour, and the beautiful summer flowers (which appear at leaf-axils) are cream coloured, marked radially with rich butterscotch yellow. The stamens are orange. Unlike Camellias, the blooms do not fall in a single piece — green sepals remain for a time on the tree and can be mistaken for unopened buds.

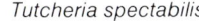

Tutcheria spectabilis

Viburnum opulus sterile
Guelder Rose

VIBURNUM

Snowball Tree,
Guelder Rose,
Sweet Viburnum Tree
* **Deciduous-evergreen/fast**
* **Spring/fragrant**
* **Ht: 5-7m/15-20ft** [C] [T]

Fragrant-flowered relatives of the Honeysuckle, enchanting **Viburnums** include a tremendous range of showy plants, all native to the cooler climates of the northern hemisphere, and welcome worldwide in temperate gardens.

The great majority of two hundred-odd species are shrubs, but several so frequently overstep the dividing line they can rightly be classed as trees.

First among them is the gorgeous Guelder Rose, **V. opulus,** which is familiar in one variety or another in parts of North Africa, Europe and northern Asia. Growing to 5m and more, it is an attractively deciduous tree with large three-lobed leaves that colour marvellously in cold areas. Its spring flower display consists of Hydrangea-like white blossoms, and in the preferred variety **V. o. sterile,** these are formed into great 15cm globular clusters that have suggested the popular name Snowball Tree.

Equally attractive in the warmer climate is evergreen Chinese species **V. odoratissimum,** the Sweet Viburnum Tree. This has an interesting spreading shape, rather wider than its height of 7m. The leaves are simple, shiny and leathery, and the late spring or early summer flower display is reminiscent of white Lilac.

Viburnums need water and a good rich soil to look happy and flower well. They are usually propagated from cuttings of half-ripened wood.

VIRGILIA

Keurboom
* **Evergreen/fast**
* **Late spring-autumn**
* **Ht: to 10m/30ft**

Here is a charming small tree from South Africa guaranteed to grow faster than anything else in the warm climate garden! Known as **keurboom** to the early Dutch settlers on the Cape, botanists have christened it **Virgilia capensis.**

Among the most important trees for a new garden, it may grow 2m in a year. Though its useful life may be only a decade, it helps fill in spaces until the main planting is established, and can be eye-catching in almost any season.

Virgilia grows to 10m and has small grey-green compound leaves. From late spring onwards, these make a splendid contrast to the profuse display of mauve-pink blossom. This is made up of literally thousands of fingernail-sized pea flowers, many of which are followed by brown pea pods.

Virgilia prefers a light, open soil. The only problem is, it is inclined to be shallow-rooted and can do with staking in exposed positions, at least until it is well established. Keep up the water during summer, and the flower display may continue into autumn.

Virgilia capensis
Keurboom

Vitex trifolia
Blue Vitex

VITEX

Blue Vitex, Chaste Tree
* **Evergreen**/fast
* **Summer**/aromatic
* **Ht: to 6m/20ft** [T] [H]

Vitex is a large genus (over 250 species) of trees and shrubs in the Verbena family, mostly native to subtropical areas of all continents. Several are grown as ornamentals, for their aromatic foliage and the showy panicles of bloom resembling **Buddleia.** They thrive in good soil, can be raised from seed, cuttings or layers.

Popular garden species include the Chaste Tree, **V. agnus-castus,** which has leaves with 5-7 woolly-backed leaflets and 30cm panicles of lilac bloom.

V. trifolia, the Blue Vitex from Asia and Australia, is a shrubby low-branching tree with mauve-tinted foliage. Each leaf consists of three leaflets; young growth is purple. The lavender-blue flowers borne in 12.5cm trusses resemble Lilac.

The New Zealand Chaste Tree or Puriri **(V. lucens)** is grown in coastal areas. It has pink flowers, may reach 20m. Other tree forms are found in South-East Asia.

INDEX

A *Acacia* 11, 13, 14, 15
Acmena, see *Syzygium* 147
Aesculus 16
African Tulip Tree, see *Spathodea* 143
Agonis 17
Alberta 17
Albizzia 18, 19
Alectryon 19
Aleurites 20
Almond, see *Prunus* 129
Almond Cherry, see *Prunus* 129
Amherstia 20
Angel's Trumpets, see *Brugmansia* 35
Angophora 21
Annatto, see *Bixa* 29
Apple, see *Malus* 108
Apple Blossom Cassia, see *Cassia* 49
Apple Gum, see *Angophora* 21
Apricot, see *Prunus* 129
Arbutus 22
Asoka, see *Saraca* 138
Australian Ash, see *Flindersia* 85
Australian White Cedar, see *Melia* 111
Azara 23
B *Backhousia* 23
Bacurubu, see *Schizolobium* 139
Banana Shrub, see *Michelia* 114
Banksia 24, 25
Barbadoes Flower Fence, see *Caesalpinia* 38
Barbadoes Pride, see *Caesalpinia* 38
Barklya 26
Barrigon, see *Bombax* 30
Bastard Sandalwood, see *Myoporum* 116
Baton du Sorcier, see *Spathodea* 143
Batswing Coral, see *Erythrina* 76
Bauhinia 27, 28, 29
Bayur Tree, see *Pterospermum* 113
Be-Still Tree, see *Thevetia* 150
Bird Lime Tree, see *Cordia* 62
Bixa 29
Black Bean, see *Castanospermum* 52
Black Locust Tree, see *Robinia* 136
Black Wattle, see *Acacia* 13
Blackwattle, see *Callicoma* 39
Blue Haze Tree, see *Jacaranda* 94
Blue Lillypilly, see *Syzygium* 147
Blue Olive Berry, see *Elaeocarpus* 75
Blue Vitex, see *Vitex* 156
Blueberry Ash, see *Elaeocarpus* 75
Bombax 30
Boobialla, see *Myoporum* 116
Bottlebrush, see *Callistemon* 40
Bracelet Honeymyrtle, see *Melaleuca* 110
Brachychiton 31, 32
Brassaia 33
Brazilwood, see *Caesalpinia* 38
Broadleaf Paperbark, see *Melaleuca* 110
Brownea 34
Brugmansia 35
Brush Box, see *Tristania* 152
Brush Cherry, see *Syzygium* 147

INDEX • 157

Brush Turpentine, see *Choricarpia* 58
Buckinghamia 36
Bull Banksia, see *Banksia* 24
Bull Bay, see *Magnolia* 104
Bumpy Ash, see *Flindersia* 85
Butea 37
Buttercup Tree, see *Cochlospermum* 60

C Cabbage Tree, see *Cordyline* 63
Caesalpinia 38
Cajeput Tree, see *Melaleuca* 110
California Privet, see *Ligustrum* 102
California Strawberry Tree, see *Arbutus* 22
Callicoma 39
Callistemon 40, 41
Calodendron 42
Camellia 43, 44, 45
Camptotheca 46
Cananga 47
Candlenut, see *Aleurites* 20
Cannonball Tree, see *Couroupita* 66
Cape Chestnut, see *Calodendron* 42
Cape Wattle, see *Albizzia* 18
Caper Tree, see *Capparis* 48
Capparis 48
Cassia 49, 50, 51
Castanospermum 52
Catalpa 53
Catawba, see *Catalpa* 53
Cat's Whisker, see *Capparis* 48
Caucasian Wingnut, see *Pterocarya* 133
Cedar Wattle, see *Acacia* 13
Ceratopetalum 54, 55
Cerbera 55
Cercis 56
Ceylon Rosewood, see *Albizzia* 19
Cham-pak, see *Michelia* 114
Champara, see *Rhodoleia* 135
Chaste Tree, see *Vitex* 156
Cherry, see *Prunus* 129
Cherry Alder, see *Syzygium* 147
Cherry Laurel, see *Prunus* 129
Cherry Plum, see *Prunus* 129
Chinaberry, see *Melia* 111
Chinese Crepe Myrtle, see *Lagerstroemia* 99
Chinese Daphne, see *Pittosporum* 123
Chinese Fringe Tree, see *Chionanthus* 57
Chinese Hawthorn, see *Photinia* 122
Chinese Privet, see *Ligustrum* 102
Chinese Redband, see *Cercis* 56
Chinese Rose, see *Camellia* 43
Chinese Silverberry, see *Elaeagnus* 75
Chinese Tulip Tree, see *Magnolia* 104
Chionanthus 57
Chiranthodendron 57
Choricarpia 58
Chorisia 58, 59
Christmas Bush, see *Ceratopetalum* 54
Cigar Cassia, see *Cassia* 49
Cigar Tree, see *Catalpa* 53
Clove, see *Syzygium* 147
Coachwood, see *Ceratopetalum* 54
Coast Myall, see *Acacia* 13
Coastal Banksia, see *Banksia* 24
Coastal Tea Tree, see *Leptospermum* 101

Cochlospermum 60
Cockscomb Coral, see *Erythrina* 76
Comarostaphylis 61
Common Hawthorn, see *Crataegus* 67
Common Pear, see *Pyrus* 134
Cootamundra Wattle, see *Acacia* 13
Coral Bean, see *Erythrina* 76
Coral Gum, see *Eucalyptus* 80
Coral Tree, see *Erythrina* 76
Corallodendron, see *Erythrina* 76
Cordia 62, 63
Cordyline 63
Cornel, see *Cornus* 64
Cornelian Cherry, see *Cornus* 64
Cornus 64, 65
Cottonwood, see *Hibiscus* 91
Couroupita 66
Crabapple, see *Malus* 108
Crataegus 67
Cream Bottlebrush, see *Callistemon* 40
Crepe Myrtle, see *Lagerstroemia* 99
Crimson Bottlebrush, see *Callistemon* 40
Crow's Ash, see *Flindersia* 85

D *Dais* 68
Damson, see *Prunus* 129
Datura, see *Brugmansia* 35
Davidia 69
Delonix 70, 71
Dhak Tree, see *Butea* 37
Diploglottis 72
Dogwood, see *Cornus* 64
Dombeya 73
Dove Tree, see *Davidia* 69
Drimys 74
Dwarf Apple Gum, see *Angophora* 21
Dwarf Poinciana, see *Caesalpinia* 38

E *Elaeagnus* 75
Elaeocarpus 75
English Hawthorn, see *Crataegus* 67
Eriobotyra 76
Erythrina 77, 78, 79
Eucalypt, see *Eucalyptus* 80
Eucalyptus 80, 81, 82, 83
Eugenia, see *Syzygium* 147
European Crab, see *Malus* 108

F *Fagraea* 84
Fern Tree, see *Jacaranda* 94
Fire Tree, see *Nuytsia* 118, see *Oreocallis* 118
Fire Wheel Tree, see *Stenocarpus* 144
Flamboyant, see *Delonix* 70
Flame of the Forest, see *Butea* 37
Flindersia 85
Floss Silk Tree, see *Chorisia* 58
Flowering Almond, see *Prunus* 129
Flowering Apricot, see *Prunus* 129
Flowering Cherry, see *Prunus* 129
Flowering Cypress, see *Tamarix* 149
Flowering Dogwood, see *Cornus* 64
Flowering Peach, see *Prunus* 129
Flowering Plum, see *Prunus* 129
Fortune's Paulownia, see *Paulownia* 120
Frangipani, see *Plumeria* 125
Fremontodendron 86
Frijolito, see *Sophora* 141

158 • FLOWERING TREES

    Fringe Tree, see *Chionanthus* 57
    Fuchsia 87
G Gean, see *Prunus* 129
    Geiger Tree, see *Cordia* 62
    Geijera 88
    Ghost Tree, see *Davidia* 69
    Giant Dogwood, see *Cornus* 64
    Gliricidia 88
    Gold Blossom Tree, see *Barklya* 26
    Golden Bough, see *Nuytsia* 118
    Golden Chain Tree, see *Laburnum* 98
    Golden Rain Tree, see *Koelreuteria* 97
    Golden Shower Tree, see *Cassia* 49
    Golden Trumpet Tree, see *Tabebuia* 148
    Golden Wattle, see *Acacia* 13
    Golden Wonder Tree, see *Cassia* 49
    Goose Plum, see *Prunus* 129
    Gordonia 89
    Graveyard Tree, see *Plumeria* 125
    Green Cherry, see *Prunus* 129
    Greengage, see *Prunus* 129
    Grevillea 90
    Guelder Rose, see *Viburnum* 154
    Guest Tree, see *Kleinhovia* 96
    Gum Myrtle, see *Angophora* 21
    Gum Tree, see *Eucalyptus* 80
    Gungunnu, see *Eucalyptus* 80
H *Hakea* 91
    Halobagat, see *Capparis* 48
    Handkerchief Tree, see *Davidia* 69
    Hau, see *Hibiscus* 91
    Hawthorn, see *Crataegus* 67
    Heath-leaf Banksia, see *Banksia* 24
    Heliotrope, see *Messerschmidia* 112
    Hibiscus 91
    Hinau, see *Elaeocarpus* 75
    Ho'awa, see *Pittosporum* 123
    Hollyleaf Sweetspire, see *Itea* 93
    Honeysuckle, see *Banksia* 24
    Hong Kong Orchid Tree, see *Bauhinia* 27
    Horse Chestnut, see *Aesculus* 16
    Hymenosporum 92
I Illawarra Flame, see *Brachychiton* 31
    Illyarie, see *Eucalyptus* 80
    Indian Bean, see *Catalpa* 53
    Indian Coral Bean, see *Erythrina* 76
    Indian Pear, see *Pyrus* 134
    Ipomoea 93
    Irish Strawberry, see *Arbutus* 22
    Ironwood, see *Metrosideros* 112
    Itea 93
    Ivory Curl Tree, see *Buckinghamia* 36
J *Jacaranda* 94
    Jamaica Caper Tree, see *Capparis* 48
    Japan Wood-oil Tree, see *Aleurites* 20
    Japanese Crab, see *Malus* 108
    Japanese Dogwood, see *Cornus* 64
    Japanese Medlar, see *Eriobotrya* 76
    Japanese Plum, see *Prunus* 129
    Japanese Stewartia, see *Stewartia* 146
    Japonica, see *Camellia* 43
    Jatropha 95
    Jerusalem Thorn, see *Parkinsonia* 120
    Judas Tree, see *Cercis* 56
    Jumbu, see *Syzygium* 147

K Kaffirboom, see *Erythrina* 76
    Kanooka, see *Tristania* 152
    Keurboom, see *Virgilia* 155
    Kigelia 96
    Kleinhovia 96
    Koelreuteria 97
    Kopsia 97
    Kou, see *Cordia* 62
    Kowhai, see *Sophora* 141
    Kukui, see *Aleurites* 20
    Kurrajong, see *Brachychiton* 31
L *Laburnum* 98
    Lacebark, see *Brachychiton* 31
    Lagerstroemia 99, 100
    Lagunaria 100
    Lecheso, see *Stemmadenia* 144
    Lemon-scented Myrtle, see *Backhousia* 23
    Lemon-scented Tea Tree, see *Leptospermum* 101
    Leopard Tree, see *Caesalpinia* 38
    Leopardwood, see *Flindersia* 85
    Leptospermum 101
    Ligustrum 102
    Lillypilly, see *Syzygium* 147
    Lily Magnolia, see *Magnolia* 104
    Lipstick Tree, see *Bixa* 29
    Liriodendron 103
    Litsea, see *Neolitsea* 117
    Lophostemon, see *Tristania* 152
    Loquat, see *Eriobotrya* 76
M Madre de Cacao, see *Gliricidia* 88
    Madrone, see *Arbutus* 22
    Magnolia 104, 105, 106, 107
    Malay Apple, see *Syzygium* 147
    Mallet Flower, see *Tupidanthus* 153
    Malus 108, 109
    Mamane, see *Sophora* 141
    Manuka, see *Leptospermum* 101
    Maximiliana, see *Cochlospermum* 60
    May, see *Crataegus* 67
    Melaleuca 110, 111
    Melia 111
    Messerschmidia 112
    Metrosideros 112, 113
    Mexican Hand Tree, see *Chiranthodendron* 57
    Mexican Palo Verde, see *Parkinsonia* 120
    Mexican Rose, see *Dombeya* 73
    Michelia 114, 115
    Mimosa, see *Acacia* 13
    Mockorange, see *Pittosporum* 123
    Monkey-hand Tree, see *Chiranthodendron* 57
    Moreton Bay Chestnut, see *Castanospermum* 52
    Morning Glory Tree, see *Ipomoea* 93
    Mountain Ebony, see *Bauhinia* 27, 29
    Mountain Jacaranda, see *Paulownia* 120
    Mt Fuji Cherry, see *Prunus* 129
    Mu-oil Tree, see *Aleurites* 20
    Myoporum 116
    Myrtus, see *Syzygium* 147
N Nanking Cherry, see *Prunus* 129
    Narrow-leaf Ironbark, see *Eucalyptus* 80
    Natal Cherry, see *Dombeya* 73
    Native Daphne, see *Pittosporum* 123
    Native Frangipani, see *Hymenosporum* 92
    Native Hazel, see *Pomaderris* 128

INDEX

O

Native Quince, see *Alectryon* 19
Native Tamarind, see *Diploglottis* 72
Needle-flower Tree, see *Posoqueria* 128
Neolitsea 117
Ngaio, see *Myoporum* 116
Norfolk Island Hibiscus, see *Lagunaria* 100
Northern Rata, see *Metrosideros* 112
N.S.W. Christmas Bush, see *Ceratopetalum* 54
Nuytsia 118
N.Z. Chaste Tree, see *Vitex* 156
Octopus Tree, see *Brassaia* 33
Ohi'a Lehua, see *Metrosideros* 112
Old Man's Beard, see *Chionanthus* 57
Oleaster, see *Elaeagnus* 75
Orchid Tree, see *Bauhinia* 27
Oreocallis 118
Oxydendron 119

P

Pagoda Tree, see *Sophora* 141
Pak-lan, see *Michelia* 114
Palm Lily, see *Cordyline* 63
Palo Blanco, see *Ipomoea* 93
Panama Flame, see *Brownea* 34
Paperbark, see *Melaleuca* 110
Parkinsonia 120
Paulownia 120, 121
Peach, see *Prunus* 129
Pear, see *Pyrus* 134
Peebeen, see *Syncarpia* 146
Peltophorum 121
Peppermint, see *Agonis* 17
Peregrina, see *Jatropha* 95
Perfume Tree, see *Cananga* 47
Persian Lilac, see *Melia* 111
Persian Silk Tree, see *Albizzia* 18
Philippine Caper Tree, see *Capparis* 48
Photinia 122
Phyllocladyx, see *Syzygium* 147
Pigeonberry Ash, see *Elaeocarpus* 75
Pincushion Tree, see *Hakea* 91
Pink Kurrajong, see *Brachychiton* 31
Pink-flowered Whitewood, see *Eucalyptus* 80
Pittosporum 123, 124
Plum, see *Prunus* 129
Plumeria 125, 126, 127
Pohutukawa, see *Metrosideros* 112
Poinciana, see *Delonix* 70
Pomaderris 128
Portugal Laurel, see *Prunus* 129
Portwine Magnolia, see *Michelia* 114
Posoqueria 128
Potato Tree, see *Solanum* 141
Prairie Crab, see *Malus* 108
Pride of Bolivia, see *Tipuana* 151
Pride of Burma, see *Amherstia* 20
Pride of China, see *Koelreuteria* 97
Pride of India, see *Lagerstroemia* 99, see *Melia* 111
Princess Tree, see *Paulownia* 120
Privet, see *Ligustrum* 102
Prunus 129, 130, 131, 132
Pterocarya 133
Pterospermum 133, 134
Pua Keni-keni, see *Fagraea* 84
Pudding-pipe Tree, see *Cassia* 49
Pulas, see *Butea* 37

Q

Puriri, see *Vitex* 156
Purple Crab, see *Malus* 108
Purple-leafed Plum, see *Prunus* 129
Pyramid Tree, see *Lagunaria* 100
Pyrus 134
Queen Crepe Myrtle, see *Lagerstroemia* 99
Queensland Lacebark, see *Brachychiton* 31
Queensland Umbrella Tree, see *Brassaia* 33

R

Rainbow Shower, see *Cassia* 49
Rata, see *Metrosideros* 112
Red Bush, see *Ceratopetalum* 54
Red Datura, see *Brugmansia* 35
Red Honeysuckle, see *Banksia* 24
Red Plum, see *Prunus* 129
Red Silk Cotton Tree, see *Bombax* 30
Red Silky Oak, see *Oreocallis* 118
Redbud, see *Cercis* 56
Redbush, see *Ceratopetalum* 54
Red-flowering Gum, see *Eucalyptus* 80
Rhodoleia 135
River Red Gum, see *Eucalyptus* 80
Robinia 136
Roblé Blanco, see *Tabebuia* 148
Rose Apple, see *Syzygium* 147
Rose Bay, see *Jatropha* 95
Rose Gum, see *Eucalyptus* 80
Rose of Venezuela, see *Brownea* 34
Rosebud Cherry, see *Prunus* 129
Rosy Trumpet Tree, see *Tabebuia* 148
Rothmannia 137
Royal Poinciana, see *Delonix* 70

S

Salt Cedar, see *Tamarix* 149
Sappanwood, see *Caesalpinia* 38
Saraca 138
Sasanqua, see *Camellia* 43
Sausage Tree, see *Kigelia* 96
Scarlet Flame Bean, see *Brownea* 34
Schefflera 139
Schizolobium 139
Sea Apple, see *Syzygium* 147
Sea Mango, see *Cerbera* 55
Sea Urchin, see *Hakea* 91
Senna Tree, see *Cassia* 49
Sesbania 140
Shaving Brush Tree, see *Bombax* 30
Shower Tree, see *Cassia* 49
Silk Cotton Tree, see *Bombax* 30
Silk Rose, see *Rhodoleia* 135
Silk Tree, see *Albizzia* 18
Silky Oak, see *Grevillea* 90
Silver Ash, see *Flindersia* 85
Silver Quandong, see *Elaeocarpus* 75
Silver Tarata, see *Pittosporum* 123
Silverberry, see *Elaegnus* 75
Singapore Shower, see *Cassia* 49
Singapore White Plumeria, see *Plumeria* 125
Siris, see *Albizzia* 18
Sloe, see *Prunus* 129
Smooth-barked Apple Gum, see *Angophora* 21
Snow Gum, see *Eucalyptus* 80
Snow in Summer, see *Melaleuca* 110
Snowball Tree, see *Viburnum* 154
Solanum 141
Sophora 141, 142
Sorrel Tree, see *Oxydendrum* 119

Soulange-Bodin's Magnolia, see *Magnolia* 104
Sourwood, see *Oxydendrum* 119
South African Daphne, see *Dais* 68
Southern Magnolia, see *Magnolia* 104
Spathodea 143
Spiny Chorisia, see *Chorisia* 58
St Lucie Cherry, see *Prunus* 129
St Thomas' Tree, see *Bauhinia* 27
Stemmadenia 14
Stenocarpus 144, 145
Stewartia 146
Summer Holly, see *Comarostaphylis* 61
Sweet Verbena Tree, see *Backhousia* 23
Sweet Viburnum, see *Viburnum* 154
Sweet Shade, see *Hymenosporum* 92
Sweetspire, see *Itea* 93
Sydney Golden Wattle, see *Acacia* 13
Syncarpia 146
Syzygium 147
Tabebuia 148
Tahinu, see *Messerschmidia* 112
Tainui, see *Pomaderris* 128
Taiwan Cherry, see *Prunus* 129
Tallow-wood, see *Eucalyptus* 80
Tamarisk, see *Tamarix* 149
Tamarix 149
Tambookie Thorn, see *Erythrina* 76
Tara, see *Caesalpinia* 38
Tea Tree, see *Leptospermum* 101
Tecoma 149
Temple Flower, see *Plumeria* 125
Ten Cent Flower, see *Fagraea* 84
Texas Umbrella Tree, see *Melia* 111
Thevetia 150
Tiger Claw, see *Erythrina* 76
Tipuana 151
Titi see *Oxydendrum* 119
Titoki, see *Alectryon* 19
Tree Fuchsia, see *Fuchsia* 87
Tree Gardenia, see *Rothmannia* 137
Tree Heliotrope, see *Messerschmidia* 112
Tree Hibiscus, see *Hibiscus* 91
Tree Poppy, see *Fremontodendron* 86
Tree Waratah, see *Oreocallis* 118
Tristania 152
Tristaniopsis, see *Tristania* 152
Trumpet Tree, see *Tabebuia* 148
Tulip Poplar, see *Liriodendron* 103

Tulip Tree, see *Liriodendron* 103
Tung-oil Tree, see *Aleurites* 20
Tupidanthus 153
Turpentine, see *Syncarpia* 146
Tutcheria 153

U Umbrella Tree, see *Brassaia* 33
   see *Melia* 111

V Variegated Ironwood, see *Metrosideros* 112
   Variegated Tiger Claw, see *Erythrina* 76
   Vegetable Humming Bird, see *Sesbania* 140
   Veitch's Magnolia, see *Magnolia* 104
   Versailles Laurel, see *Prunus* 129
   Viburnum 154
   Victorian Box, see *Pittosporum* 123
   Virgilia 155
   Vitex 156

W Water Gum, see *Tristania* 152
   Water Myrtle, see *Syzygium* 147
   Wattle, see *Acacia* 13
   Weeping Bottlebrush, see *Callistemon* 40
   Weeping Cherry, see *Prunus* 129
   Weeping Myrtle, see *Syzygium* 147
   Wheel of Fire, see *Streptocarpus* 144
   White Bottlebrush, see *Callistemon* 40
   White Cedar, see *Melia* 111
      see *Tabebuia* 149
   White Dogwood, see *Cornus* 64
   White Orchid Tree, see *Bauhinia* 27
   Wild Olive, see *Elaeagnus* 75
   Wild Pear, see *Dombeya* 73
      see *Pyrus* 134
   Wilga, see *Geijera* 88
   Willow Bottlebrush, see *Callistemon* 40
   Willow Myrtle, see *Agonis* 17
   Willow Pittosporum, see *Pittosporum* 123
   Willow-leaf Pear, see *Pyrus* 134
   Winter's Bark, see *Drimys* 74
   Woman's Tongue Tree, see *Albizzia* 18
   Wong-lan, see *Michelia* 114

Y Yelow Bells, see *Tecoma* 149
   Yellow Elder, see *Tecoma* 149
   Yellow Flame, see *Peltophorum* 121
   Yellow Jacaranda, see *Schizolobium* 139
   Yellow Oleander, see *Thevetia* 150
   Yellow Poinciana, see *Peltophorum* 121
   Ylang Ylang, see *Cananga* 47
   Yulan, see *Magnolia* 104